Clive Paine was born and educated in Bury St Edmunds and apart from years at University, has worked there all his life. He is a teacher, lecturer, author and broadcaster on all aspects of local history. He has taught history and local history for nearly 30 years, 21 of which have been as County Advisory Teacher for Archives and Local History in Suffolk. He has been a part time lecturer in Local History for the Cambridge University Institute of Continuing Education for over twenty years.

His publications include *Hartest: A Village History; The Culford Estate; The History of Eye; The Spoil of Melford Church* (with David Dymond); *Bury St. Edmunds* and *Francis Frith's Suffolk*

He frequently broadcasts on local and national radio and appeared with Prince Edward on his 'Crown and Country' series for ITV and has been profiled in *Reader's Digest*. He is a Council member of the Suffolk Institute of Archaeology and History; the executive of the Suffolk Local History Council and past Chairman of the Education Committee of the British Association for Local History. He is also a Lay Reader at St. Mary's in Bury.

SUFFOLK BEDSIDE BOOK

A Collection of Prose and Poetry

SELECTED AND INTRODUCED BY
CLIVE PAINE

THE DOVECOTE PRESS

This book is in memory of my wife Dorothy,
who died 9th March 1999.
Dorothy Elizabeth Goddard was born at Botesdale, into the extensive and
interwoven Brethren and Baptist farming families of High Suffolk.
Her roots in the clay soil and in unadorned nonconformity, where Jesus
was proclaimed, at 'The Meeting,' by farmers and agricultural labourers,
gave her a deep knowledge of the dialect and an instinctive,
yet no-nonsense appreciation of both
the people and landscape of Suffolk.
Members of her extended family were included in the writings of Revd
Richard Cobbold, Doreen Wallace, Adrian Bell and Ronald Blyth.

First published in 2002 by The Dovecote Press Ltd
Stanbridge, Wimborne, Dorset BH21 4JD

ISBN 1 904349 06 4

© Introductions, Clive Paine 2002

Typeset in Monotype Sabon
Printed and bound in Singapore

A CIP catalogue record for this book is available
from the British Library

1 3 5 7 9 8 6 4 2

CONTENTS

INTRODUCTION

As the title suggests this is a book to be read late at night, or in the early hours of the morning. However, it is not intended to be a substitute for sleeping pills or a spouse.

It is hoped that this collection of extracts and epitaphs gives an insight into various aspects of life in Suffolk over the past 500 years. Contributions have been taken from local and national poets, travellers, social and economic writers and authors, who found their inspiration in the vast skies and ever-changing landscape of the county. Several pieces are in the delightful Suffolk dialect, which is not as easy to imitate as Norfolk and, always defeats the best efforts of actors and people from 'the Shires'.

Most of the sources quoted are available at the three branches of the Suffolk Record office where the ever-helpful staff will be delighted to help with further research on any aspect of Suffolk's past.

I have to confess that these are my own favourite pieces, many of which I have used in performances and talks over the years. My hope is that whether you, like me, have your family roots in Suffolk-soil, or are newly arrived, since Suffolk was 'discovered' by the Greater London Council in the 1960s, or are just visiting, will find much to delight and amuse, but not to lie awake worrying about, in this selection.

I wish to thank my friends Barbara Caruth, Mel Spurling, Jean Turner and Peter Northeast, for their generous help in suggesting items for this collection. But above all, I have to thank Pat Murrell for her never-ending flow of advice and sources. However, none of this would have been possible without Jane Cummins and David Caruth. Jane produced the typescript from sources in medieval and Tudor English, Suffolk dialect and my handwriting, which requires a palaeography course in itself; David read the draft, corrected the typescript and suggested improvements to the overall text. Any mistakes in matters of detail are, of course, mine alone.

CLIVE PAINE, October 2002

I · LANDSCAPE AND CHARACTER

An Intimate Landscape

The natural landscape of Suffolk is, before all else, undramatic and soft. This is not a country of grand vistas as from Hay Tor on Dartmoor, the Wrekin in Shropshire or Sutton Bank in Yorkshire. Admittedly, a few long views can be found. Many of us, for example, have enjoyed that curving sweep of shingled coastline from the cliff at Dunwich; or have gazed admiringly from Warren Hall on the edge of Newmarket, across intensively farmed fens towards the silver-tipped silhouette of Ely Cathedral. In general, however, the absence of mountains, great ranges of hills and dramatic escarpments means that panoramas are rare. When walking or driving through Suffolk, one does not normally see further than three miles, and often less than one mile. As a result the view is constantly changing, and changing totally, in a way that does not happen when one walks, for instance, along Wensleydale or on the slopes of Helvellyn. Visibility of course changes with the seasons, and one of the delights of walking in Suffolk during winter is to see something which is normally masked by leaves. But the range is nearly always fairly short, and the view usually enclosed by nearby ridges, hills or simply trees. Beyond that limited horizon our eyes are launched into the vast East Anglian sky where mountainous clouds often, if only fleetingly, display all the breadth and majesty which are lacking in the gentle scene below.

In fact, the natural undulations of the landscape are often so subtle that many visitors, even residents, are not even conscious of them. They write off Suffolk as 'flat', as Noel Coward did Norfolk. Of course, the country does have its flat plateaux, around Mendlesham airfield for instance, but many of us don't notice how frequently we climb out of a village, and over a ridge before dropping down to the next village, just as one does, but more laboriously, in Devon or Westmorland. And as we hurtle in top gear along the A 45, [A 14] many of us are not aware of crossing that highly significant watershed by Haughley Park, which divides the eastern part of Suffolk draining towards the North Sea from the western part draining towards the Wash.

A very important consequence of the small-scale, intimate character of the natural countryside is that certain features which would be overshadowed or lost in grander landscapes gain a special prominence in Suffolk: for example, church towers, woods, hedgerows, individual trees, barns, silos, battery-houses, lines of pylons. In this relatively soft fertile region which for well over a thousand years has been densely settled and intensively farmed, virtually everything, including the wood and heaths, is made by man, or determined by him, for good economic and functional reasons. In no other county of England is man's contribution so important visually, whatever its character or date.

David Dymond, 'The Landscape', Suffolk For Ever, (1989), pp. 19-21.
Celia Jennings (ed)

Suffolk

While poets in bright fantasy delight,
Or for a theme to foreign fields take flight,
I choose thee, Suffolk ! with thy piercing breeze,
Thy well-form'd team-horse, porkers, malt and cheese,
Whose virtues all thy native bard set forth,
Nor have they lost an atom of their worth;

But since his time have Suffolk men unfurl'd
Improvement's flag, and given to the world
Of agricultural instruments whose fame
Have won for thee a never-dying fame.

To thy bleak shore and health-bestowing air,
From distant parts right many now repair:
Lowestoft, once for nought but fishing gear
Renown'd, now owns its terraces and pier;
And Aldborough and ancient Southwold, each
Can boast attractions on its rugged beach;
And, farther south, full well do tourists know
Brave Landguard Fort and pretty Felixstow,
Whence on to Ipswich flows the river's tide,
'Twixt lovely spots which smile on either side;
Here Woolverstone delights the passer's eye –
Here Nacton's oaks their branches wave on high.

Nacton ! than thee flat Suffolk cannot boast
A sweeter village on her sandy coast.
Thy 'Hall' thy 'Park', both picturesque and grand,
Half hid by foliage on fair Orwell's strand;
Thy yellow whins and spreading chestnut-trees,
Which swell thy beauties and perfume the breeze;
Thy mossy church, the poorhouse on the mound;
Thy thick-grown covert, where at eve resound
The nightingale's soft warblings, and the crow
Of pheasant-cocks as to their roosts they go –
All tend to make thee Nacton, what thou art,
Fit scene to charm the bard of Nature's heart.

Nor, quiet Dunwich ! must thou be forgot,
(By pleasure-folk a much-frequented spot),
Once ranking chief 'mong cities of the East,
Now of our sea-side villages the least;
For all thy grandeur, which in days of yore
Was meet for monarchs, now is seen no more;
All by that mighty despot, Neptune, ta'en,

And buried in the sands of his domain.
And even yet, when from the rough north-west
The blustering wind disturbs the ocean's breast,
The seething waves their foam-crown'd heads uplift,
And batter down thy rotten yielding clift:
Still, charms e'en now are found thy shades among,
In praise of which well thy own poet sung.
Yes ! Suffolk, much I prize thy fertile soil,
Land of true enterprise and honest toil !

John Lushington, A New Year's Budget, (1866), pp. 8–10.
[Suffolk's 'own poet' referred to in the third line from the end may be Robert Bloomfield, Bernard Barton, James Bird or George Crabbe]

The Climate

Arthur Young of Bradfield Combust, President of the Board of Agriculture, leading advocate of enclosure and agricultural improvements, notes the effect of climate on agriculture.

It is unquestionably one of the driest climates in the kingdom; with which circumstance two others unite: the frosts are severe, and the N. E. winds, in the spring, sharp and prevalent . . . Severe winters and dry springs have a strong influence on agriculture: the former renders turnips a precarious dependence, and the latter lengthen the winter, to the great expence of the keepers of livestock. On the whole, however, the climate of this county must be reckoned favourably.

Arthur Young, A General View of the Agriculture of Suffolk, (1794) p. 2.

Commodities and Incommodities of Suffolk: 1603

Robert Reyce, gentleman, of Preston, near Lavenham, outlines the advantages and disadvantages of Suffolk as a coastal county. However dry the climate, Reyce relies on the clay soil and bad roads to impede an invasion.

It is not amongst the least, for which this shire is indebted to nature, to receive so fitt a scituation, that so quickly and commodiously it can vent and make returne of such commodities which it affordeth, for if navigable ryvers, diversitie of commodious havens, for exportation and importation, neernesse vnto the quickest and readiest markets of best trade, and with as little pirrill and small charge as any other shire may be justly acknowledged the sole means of a profitable and commodious scituation, then shall this shire ot all such as truly know it, justly deserve that true commendation. I must confesse as all other earthly benefits are accompanied with some incommodities, for it is objecteth it lyeth open and is ready for forreigne invasion, there bee so many havens, harbours, creekes, and other places of ready discent, that the enemy is soon entered . . .

Butt that which is common to all other sea bordering shires ought nott here to bee reckned as a perticuler incommoditie, neither may those furtive assaults, with a more momentary returne bee reputed as a warlike invasion, which whensoever it shall bee effected, by that time the invaders meet with our deep myrie soyle, our narrow and fowle lanes, our manifold inclosures, severed with so many deep ditches, hedges, and store of wood, bushes and trees, seing the impassableness of this Country, with any martiall forces, albeit there were noe other meanes of resistance, they will have just cause to repent their rashnessse

Lord Francis Hervey, (ed), Robert Reyce, The Breviary of Suffolk, *(1603),*
(1902), pp. 14–15.

The Suffolk Character

East Anglia as I have found, has some claim to be a focus of English genius. Much that is most typical in English politics and adventure, thought and science and art practice has come out of East Anglia. The people of Suffolk, sometimes apparently slow, are yet ever exuberant in energy, often bright of eye and quick of action.

Cautious, patient, pliant, conciliatory, they can yet be forceful, independent, obstinate.

Not superficially brilliant like the people of the south-west, they are not so impenetrably reserved behind a hard rind like the people of the north; there is a strong emotional undercurrent which makes itself felt, even though it may not be visible, so that they are a friendly people whom it is not difficult to get on with.

Women play a large part among them. The solidity these people of Suffolk owed to their Dutch and Flemish affinities has been modified by French Huguenot and other foreign elements. They are a practical and materialistic people who delight to make their surroundings spacious and beautiful, a religious and benevolent people, indeed, yet by no means ascetic, scarcely even , in the narrow sense, a severely moral people; their instincts in life, as in science and art, tend to direct them towards Nature.

Havelock Ellis, My Life, *(1940), p. 19.*

Suffolk and Flanders.

We rested the first night at Bury St. Edmund's, the Montpelier of England; a place no less remarkable for its ecclesiastical antiquities, than for the polished manners of its inhabitants, and the curious extraneous fossils found in its neighbourhood . . .

The journey the following day to Yarmouth, was through a district so much resembling Flanders, that nothing was wanted to make the resemblance perfect, but the fine avenues of trees adorning the Low Countries, which deserve to diversify the sameness of a level territory. Perhaps there is not a more fertile part of our island. The fields resemble extensive gardens; and everywhere, among the standing corn, or in the pasture lands, the utmost attention to neatness was visible. In the cottages, the same disposition was conspicuous; thereby providing the great attention shewn by the landlords, of the wants and wishes of their respective tenants.

Edward Clarke, Travels in Various Countries of Europe, Asia and Africa, *(1819), vol iii, p. 1–3*

From the Shires

Since the time of the Anglo Saxon Kingdom, East Anglia has felt distinct from the rest of the country. The motto of the University of East Anglia is 'Do Different.'

If one has not had the good fortune to have been born in one of the Three Counties – Norfolk, Suffolk or Essex – one comes from the Sheres, a term that seems to embrace the rest of England, not to say

Scotland and Wales as well. It used to be the worst judgment one could pass on the working qualities of a horse to say that he had 'a bit of the Sheres in him'. A similar judgment was given recently by an old native on a marriage that had turned out badly; the girl was born here and except for a brief period during the war had lived here all her life; but the man – well: 'He came from the Sheres'! And all was explained, since all products of the Sheres turned out no better than they were expected to, whether they were men, horses or merely 'grut big ol' stoons'.

But this division into the Three Counties and the rest of England has, in fact, some sort of historical sanction. Domesday Book, the 1086 survey, was originally produced in two volumes: the smaller volume was entirely devoted to Essex, Norfolk and Suffolk. Moreover the descriptions in this volume are very much more detailed than those of the larger one.

George Ewart Evans, Ask The Fellows Who Cut The Hay, *(1956), p. 78.*

Suffolk Dialect

Justin Brooke began farming at Wickhambrook in 1928 and, after thirty-four years in Suffolk, provides an amusing and affectionate analysis of the local dialect.

To understand the Suffolk character one must understand the Suffolk language. This is by no means easy for a stranger. Its grammar, which is strictly observed, differs in a marked way from that of ordinary English. Also the intonation of the voice is different. Direct statements are rare, meanings are hinted at rather than expressed, and discourse generally reflects the mind of the speaker and is muddled. Suffolkers are masters of the irrelevant and the non sequitur. Nothing is clear-cut; nothing is logical; even the pronunciation of the words varies from time to time – the word 'say' for example, can be pronounced as spelt or as the word 'sigh' or anything in between. A manager of ours was tinkering with a car. He told the boy who assisted him to get some pliers. The boy returned with a packet of Player's cigarettes.

The Suffolker lives in the present and he often uses the present tense to refer to present, past and future . . .

The word 'it' is not in the Suffolk dialect at all; the word 'that' is used instead. The third person singular never has an 's' at the end. The poet Bloomfield submitted his poem 'The Farmer's Boy' to his patron so that the grammar could be corrected before publication. His patron records that almost all he had to do was put an 's' on to every verb of the third person singular in the present tense. When spoken by one of the old inhabitants, the language has a fine rhythm and the reduction in the number of sibilants adds to its charm.

The words 'do' and 'don't' are used to mean 'if you do' and 'if you don't', hence the saying 'do don't, you ought to should'. Should here is redundant and used to intensify the meaning. Double and treble negatives are frequently used for the same purpose. A certain farmer sacked his men with the words: 'Do all of you go away now and don't none of you never come back no more.' Someone asked a farm worker where the ladder was. He replied: 'That lie agin the stack, don't that did do.'

There are three forms of the imperative-the most polite 'pray do this', the most common 'do you do this' and the bluntest 'do this'. Some words require explaining. There is a word which is usually spelt 'bor' but we spell it 'ber'. It means pal. It is pronounced in West Suffolk like the second syllable of the German word 'knabe'-there is no 'r' sound whatever, but if we spell the word without a final 'r' the reader would assume it would be part of the verb 'to be'; but please remember the 'r' is not sounded. The word is used only when addressing an equal. In the old days, when a foreman of mine addresses a worker as 'ber' the worker showed obvious signs of gratification.

The plural of the word 'ber' is the word 'together'. Thus you say, if addressing an equal, 'go you along, ber' and if you were addressing two or more equals, you would say 'go you along together', even if you meant them to go separately . . .

The adverb goes before the verb – for example, 'I am now going', not, 'I am going now'. The meaning is always hinted at rather than expressed, and the negative aspect is given, not the positive. 'I doubt it won't rain today' means it is likely to be fine. They have a curious way of telling certain times; if the time is twenty-seven minutes to two, it is stated to be five and twenty-two to two. The shed where carriages used to be put was known as the chaise-house and that where the farm cart was put the cart-lodge. A 'pightle' is a small enclosed pasture, generally used by the farmer for his 'house-cow'; a ginger tom-cat is called a 'frum'. The stranger, until he gets used to the language, often feels at a loss because thought often appears to be phrased upside down and conclusions are queer – 'I lost that glove but I knowed just where I left that and I went to the place and there that was – gone.'

In the war we had a lady doctor who came to the village. Old Hub – short for Herbert – had a bad leg and went for treatment to the surgery; she said: 'Well, pull your trousers up and let me look at your leg.' His answer was : ' I ain't never showed myself to a mawther, not since I were a little one and I ain't a-going to do that now.' Away he stumped and left nature to cure his leg. The word 'mawther' which is rare here, only means a girl; but I cannot help fearing that the lady doctor probably thought it meant something else . . .

The Suffolk saying with regard to boy labour is – and how true it is! – one is one and two's a half and three ain't nothing at all.

Justin and Edith Brooke, Suffolk Prospect, *(1963), pp. 26–31.*

The Suffolk Landscape: 1939

In aspect and outlook Suffolk seems content to amble along at least a century behind the rest of England. Because it has not been visited with the questionable comforts of modernity, it remains shy and unsophisticated. Not only are the people shy, but the spirit of the country itself is independent, capricious and elusive – if you don't treat it properly it will, like an unresponsive tortoise, retire to the seclusion of its own shell and escape you for ever. That slight animosity of Suffolk attracts the right people and repels the wrong ones.

It is a country for the individualist, for the explorer and the lover of loneliness. Most people who have merely passed through it have very little to say in its favour. The reason for this is simple: you can't judge Suffolk from a motor-car, because the main roads have the dullest landscape in the county. Whether the roads have altered the look of the countryside, or whether its dullness is purely a coincidence (providential in many ways), the fact remains that Suffolk from the main road is decidedly uninteresting. The route from London to

Norwich crosses the county by that extraordinary piece of country called Breckland, which at first sight seems nothing more than a dozen miles of dreary heath. As to the other main road, between Stratford St. Mary and Ipswich it shows the country at its worst – treeless, hedgeless and flat; between Ipswich and Saxmundham, the improvement is regrettably slight; and it is only from Yoxford to Lowestoft that the weary traveller gets a glimpse of the real, untainted Suffolk, by which time he is probably in no condition to appreciate it. But once get away from these roads for a mile or so and the dullness, even on the stretch between Stratford and Ipswich, evaporates like a morning mist. This transformation is one of the strangest, pleasantest and most startling surprises in the whole county. Unfortunately, not many people bother to experience it. They are content to condemn Suffolk without a hearing, not realizing that it will never show itself to them unless they set out to find it in the right and proper way, which is, in part, what is meant by its shyness.

You will have to look for the charm of the Suffolk countryside – it is a charm most carefully hidden. Perhaps this is because we have no downs or high hills from which you can survey the landscape at your leisure – there is just one, just 450 feet high, a few miles from Bury St. Edmunds, [at Rede] that I have vowed to make the goal of some future pilgrimage. When you can see farms and villages and woods spread out beneath you simply by sitting still and turning your head, then three-quarters of your exploration are already over. But you can't do that in Suffolk; you can never say for certain what is going to confront you round this bend in the lane or past the corner of that hedge, for the very reason that you can't see it. Suffolk is a discerning county, as full of surprises as a Christmas stocking, and I find this state of constant speculation one of its greatest delights. But don't think that we have no views at all; John Constable knew where to look for them, and he found in Suffolk some of the most beautiful in the country. And yet because he knew that the coast did not suit his brush so well as the inland valleys, and because he never painted along that land which shelves down to the sea, there were others that even he did not find.

The views are all the more pleasing because they are unexpected. Everything about Suffolk is unexpected – views, valleys, villages, cottages, farms, the castles and abbeys that have made the county an antiquarian's Utopia. You never suspect their existence until you find them accidentally. An abbey, or what is left of it, may escape you in the guise of a battered cattle-shed, or it may leap at you from the middle of a cornfield, or show you but one coy, crumbled buttress from the protection of a thick wood. As to the castles, I can best show my meaning by telling you that I know of one that had been converted into a railway-station. [Clare]

Like the country itself, the buildings are quite irregular and illogical in their placing and character. Cottages and farmhouses, even churches, often seem to exist without any human contact at all, connected with the nearest road by an almost unrecognisable and wholly impassable cart-track. On a walk of a dozen miles you will find scores of them, desolate, untended, making their last long stand against decay; to-day they seem even farther from civilisation than they were three hundred years ago, and rather than their beauty it is their stubbornness and their courage that will attract you.

Have they no link with the world? Apparently not, for the village to which they belong is probably a couple of miles away, undreamed of until you are in the midst of it. And the villages, too, are lonely – remote settlements in a remote land, with no prettiness about them, but a solid and unconventional beauty, an inward warmth distilled by the years and cloaked with an outward austerity. Popular villages are those known as picturesque; the virtues of the Suffolk villages still exist because they are as yet undiscovered by the world. In my heart I hope they never will be. 'All men kill the thing they love,' and they have succeeded in killing most of the villages of which they have grown over-fond.

Julian Tennyson, Suffolk Scene, *(1939), pp. 1-4*

The Vale of Slaughden

In 1860 Wilkie Collins stayed at Aldeburgh and later included it in his novel No Name. *His description of the desolation and isolation at Slaughden, is reminiscent of George Crabbe.*

Slowly and in silence the two walked on, until they reached the southern limit of the houses, and entered on a little wilderness of shingle and withered grass – the desolate end of Aldborough, the lonely beginning of Slaughden.

It was a dull airless evening. Eastward was the grey majesty of the sea, hushed in breathless calm; the horizon line invisibly melting into the monotonous misty sky; the idle ships shadowy and still on the idle water. Southward, the high ridge of the sea dyke, and the grim massive circle of a martello tower, reared high on its mound of grass, closed the view darkly on all that lay beyond. Westward, a lurid streak of sunset glowed red in the dreary haven – blackened the fringing trees on the far borders of the great inland marsh – and turned its little gleaming water-pools to pools of blood. Nearer to the eye, the sullen flow of the tidal river Alde, ebbed noiselessly from the muddy banks; and nearer still, lonely and unprosperous by the bleak waterside, lay the lost little port of Slaughden, with its forlorn wharfs and warehouses of decaying wood, and its few scattered coasting vessels deserted on the oozy river-shore. No fall of waves was heard on the beach; no trickling of waters bubbled audibly from the idle stream. Now and then, the cry of a seabird rose from the region of the marsh: and, at intervals, from farmhouses far in the inland waste, the faint winding of horns to call the cattle home, travelled mournfully through the evening calm.

Magdalen drew her hand from the captain's arm, and led the way to the mound of the Martello tower. 'I am weary of walking,' she said. 'Let us stop and rest here.'

Wilkie Collins, No Name, *(1862), p.272.*

2 · AGRICULTURE

The Richness of the Soil : 1603

The soyle it selfe receiveth nott in every place one certaine kind, butt in some places as among the inclosures it is heavy with clay, and sometime entermixed with chalke in other places as nearer the champion it is lighter with a sandy and variable earth, and in those clay countries where the ground is so heavie the best husbands without six strong horses in one plow will not till their land, so that generally, the country in winter time out of the common roads is very foule. Butt nature hath countervailed this defect with a naturall fatnes, and richness in the soile; whereby each part is endowed most plentifully: for those parts inclining to the east having suffiecient tillage, abound with all meadow and pasture by reason whereof their greatest commodities are raised by feeding and grasing, the other parts westward towards the champin having sufficient meddow, aboundance of tillage, and feeding of many sheep, doe from hence raise their greatest profits. The midle parts of the country are rich in pasture and plenty of meddowes butt their chiefest is corne grounds from all which riseth the gain that filleth their purses.
Lord Francis Hervey, (ed), Robert Reyce, The Breviary of Suffolk, (1603), (1902), p. 26.

Suffolk in 1724

Suffolk is blest with an Air so sweet and wholesome, that London Physicians have recommended it for the Cure of their consumptive Patients. It's well stored with Parks, well watered, and so furnished with Accommodations for Pleasure, that it is much inhabited and frequented by Gentry.

Its Soil is various; the Eastern Parts all along the Coast for five or six Miles inland, are generally heathy, sandy, full of little Hills and Springs, and bleak, though heretofore it should seem to have been very woody, by the old Saxon Names given to the Towns and Places hereabouts. The manuring of the Ground is generally for Rye, Pease, Brank, Hemp, Sheep-Walks &c. The more Inland Parts, commonly called High Suffolk, or the Wood –Lands, are pretty level, close and dirty, being clayey Ground, and chiefly employed for the dairy. The Southern Parts along the Borders of Essex, and abutting on Part of Cambridgeshire, are much of the same Nature for Pasture-Ground: Those about Bury, and from thence Northwesterly, are Champaign, abounding with excellent Corn of all sorts, except some Parts near New-Market, which is mostly green Heath.

Great Improvements have of late Years been made in this County, by sowing of Turneps to fatten Sheep with, though it is generally allowed that Mutton is not so good as others are. They have a great Trade for their Cheese, though poor and lean to a Proverb; but for Butter, it carried the Name, and not undeservedly, before that of other Counties. Some Trade they likewise have in home-spun Linen, and making Sail-Cloth, as also in Wool, and White-Work for Norwich Worsteds. The Coast has been eminent for the fishing Trade, but now much decayed to what it was, which is owing, besides other causes, chiefly to that of New-Castle.

As to its relative Condition, High Suffolk is chiefly the Seat of the Yeomanry; the Gentry are commonly seated in great Towns, the mixed Soil, the Fielding by Bury, and the Sand-Lands; and if Norfolk exceeds Suffolk in the Number of its Churches, Suffolk generally exceeds in the Handsomness of them.

Herman Moll, A New Description of England and Wales, (1724), p. 145.

Dairy Farming in High Suffolk : 1722

High-Suffolk is full of rich feeding grounds and large farms, mostly employed in dairies and making the Suffolk butter and cheese of which I have spoken already. Among these rich grounds stand some market-towns, though not of very considerable note, such as Framlingham, Beccles, Bungay etc., all on the edge of the river Waveney which parts here the counties of Suffolk and Norfolk . . . Halesworth, Saxmundham, Debenham, Aye or Eye, all standing in this eastern side of Suffolk, in which, as I have said, the whole country is employed in dairies or in feeding of cattle.

This part of England is also remarkable for being the first where the feeding and fattening of cattle, both sheep as well as black cattle, with turnips was first practised in England, which is made a very great part of the improvement of their lands to this day; and from whence the practice is spread over most of the east and south parts of England, to the great enriching of the farmers and increase of fat cattle... and a very great quantity of beef and mutton also is bought every year and every week to London from this side of England, and much more than was formerly known to be fed there.

In this part which we call High-Suffolk, there are not so many families of gentry or nobility placed as in the other side of the country, but it is observed that though their seats are not so frequent here, their estates are, and the pleasure of West Suffolk is much of it supported by the wealth of High-Suffolk, for the richness of the lands and application of the people to all kinds of improvement, is scarcely credible; also the farmers are so very considerable and their farms and dairies so large, that it is very frequent for a farmer to have a thousand pounds of stock upon his farm in cows only.

Daniel Defoe, A Tour Thro' The Whole Island of Great Britain, *(1724), pp. 58-60.*

Suffolk Cheese

Robert Bloomfield of Honington was a peasant poet, patronized by the Duke of Grafton and Capel Lofft. His Farmer's Boy *depicts the life of 'Giles' through the seasons. Suffolk Cheese was notorious for*

its close texture and hardness; often being called 'Suffolk Bang.' As
Bloomfield reveals it was the excessive skimming of the milk, leaving
no cream, that turned 'the meads sweet nectar into stone.'

Unrivall'd stands thy country Cheese, O Giles!
Whose very name alone engenders smiles;
Whose fame abroad by every tongue is spoke,
The well-known butt of many a flinty joke,
That pass like current coin the nation through;
And, ah! experience proves the satire true.
Provision's grave, thou ever craving mart,
Dependant, huge Metropolis! Where Art
Her pouring thousands stows in breathless rooms,
Midst pois'nous smokes and steams, and rattling looms;
Where Grandeur revels in unbounded stores;
Restraint, a slighted stranger at their doors!
Thou, like a whirlpool, drain'st the countries round,
Till London market, London price, resound
Through every town, round every passing load,
And dairy produce throngs the eastern road:
Delicious veal, and butter, every hour,
From Essex lowlands, and the banks of the Stour;
And further far, where numerous herds repose,
From Orwell's brink, from Weveny, or Ouse.
Hence Suffolk dairy-wives run mad for cream,
And leave their milk with nothing but its name;
Its name derision and reproach pursue,
And strangers tell of 'three times skimm'd sky-blue.'
To cheese converted, what can be its boast?
What, but the common virtues of a post!
If drought o'ertake it faster than the knife,
Most fair it bids for stubborn length of life,
And, like the oaken shelf whereon 'tis laid,
Mocks the weak efforts of the bending blade;
Or in the hog-trough rests in perfect spite,
Too big to swallow, and too hard to bite.
Inglorious victory! Ye Cheshire meads,
Or Severn's flow'ry dales, where plenty treads,

Was your rich milk to suffer wrongs like these,
Farewell your pride! farewell renowned cheese!
The skimmer dread, whose ravages alone
Thus turn the mead's sweet nectar into stone.
Robert Bloomfield, The Farmer's Boy. Spring *(1800) pp.16-18*

Suffolk Poultry for London

This county of Suffolk is particularly famous for furnishing the City of London and all the counties round, with turkeys, and that it is thought that there are more turkeys bred in this county, and the part of Norfolk that adjoins to it, than in all the rest of England . . .

I received an account from a person living on the place, viz . , that they have counted 300 droves of turkeys (for they drive them all in droves on foot) pass in one season over Stratford Bridge on the river Stour, which parts Suffolk from Essex, about six miles from Colchester on the road from Ipswich to London. These droves, as they say, generally contain from three hundred to a thousand each drove, so one may suppose them to contain 500 one with another which is 150,000 in all, and yet this is one of the least passages, the numbers which travel by New-Market-Heath and the open country and the forest, and also the numbers that come by Sudbury and Clare, being many more.

For the further supplies for the markets of London with poultry, of which these counties particularly abound, they have within these few years found it practicable to make the geese travel on foot too, as well as the turkeys, and a prodigious number are brought up to London in droves from the farthest parts of Norfolk, even from the Fen country about Lynn, Downham, Wisbich and the Washes, as also from the east side of Norfolk and Suffolk of whom it is very frequent now to meet droves with a thousand, sometimes two thousand in a drove. They begin to drive them generally in August, by which time the harvest is almost over and the geese may feed on the stubble as they go. Thus they hold on to the end of October, when the roads begin to be too stiff and deep for their broad feet and short legs to march in.

Besides these methods of driving these creatures on foot, they have of late also invented a new method of carriage, being carts formed on purpose with four stories or stages to put the creatures in one above the other, by which invention one cart will carry a very great number, and for the smoother going, they drive with two horses abreast, like a coach, so quartering the road for the ease of the gentry that thus ride; changing horses they travel night and day, so that they bring the fowls 70, 80 or 100 miles in two days and one night . . .

Daniel Defoe, A Tour Thro' The Whole Island of Great Britain, (1724), pp. 59–60

Suffolk Farming : 1825

Pollarded trees are still a feature of the Suffolk landscape, as recorded here by William Cobbett, the political activist.

The land in such a beautiful state, the farmhouses all white, and all so much alike; the barns, and everything about the homesteads so snug; the stocks of turnips so abundant everywhere; the sheep and cattle in such fine order; the wheat all drilled; the ploughman so expert; the furrows, if a quarter of a mile long, as straight as a line, and laid as truly as if with a level: in short, here is everything to delight the eye, and to make the people proud of their country; and this is the case throughout the whole of this county. I have always found Suffolk farmers great boasters of their superiority over others; and I must say that it is not without reason . . .

In those counties [East Anglia] too, there is great taste with regard to trees of every description, from the hazel to the oak. In Suffolk it appears to be just the contrary: here is the great dissight of all these three eastern counties. Almost every bank of every field is studded with pollards, that is to say, trees that have been beheaded, at from six to twelve feet from the ground, than which nothing in nature can be more ugly. They send out shoots from the head, which are lopped off once in ten or a dozen years for fuel, or other purposes. To add to the deformity, the ivy is suffered to grow on them which, at the same time, checks the growth of the shoots. These pollards become hollow very soon and, as timber, are fit for nothing but gate-posts, even before they be hollow . . . I have scarcely seen a single farm of a hundred acres without pollards sufficient to find the farm-house sufficient in fuel, without any assistance from coals, for several years.

However the great number of farm-houses in Suffolk, the neatness of those houses, the moderation in point of extent which you generally see, and the great store of the food in the turnips, and the admirable management of the whole, form a pretty good compensation for the want of beauties. The land is generally as clean as a garden ought to be; and though it varies a good deal as to lightness and stiffness, they make it all bear prodigious quantities of swedish turnips; and on them, pig, sheep, and cattle all equally thrive. I did not observe a single poor miserable animal in the whole county.

William Cobbett, Rural Rides, *Everyman Edition, (1914), pp.225–27.*

The Harvest Cart in Suffolk

John Lushington, also known as 'Quill', was Clerk to the Chief Constable. He wrote two outstanding dialect poems, which he used to perform at Harvest Suppers.

Yow, Jack, bring them 'ere hosses here –
   Get this 'ere waggin out;
I think this weather mean to clear,
   So jest yow look about !
Come, put old Jolly to, right quick –
   Now then, hook Di'mond on,
(There chuck yow down that plaguy stick !)
   An' goo an' call old John.

John bo' the 'Cart shod close' we'll try
   (Get yow upon the stack);
I'm sure the whate's by this time dry –
   Bring them 'ere forks here, Jack.
Blarm that 'ere chap ! where is he now ?
   Just look yow here, my man,
If yow don't want to have a row,
   Be steady if yow can.

Ope that 'ere gate. Wish ! Jolly – Wo !
   Cop that 'ere rope up, Sam;
Now I'll jump down an' pitch bo'; so
Jump yow up where I am.

Load wide enough, mate – that's the style –
   Now hold ye ! Di'mond ! – Wo-o !
Jack ! – that 'ere boy do me that rile –
   Just mind yow where yow goo !

There goo a rabbit ! Boxer, hi ! –
   She's sure to get to grownd,
Hold ye ! Now then bo', jest yow try
To turn them nicely round.
Don't knock them shoves down ! Blarm the boy ! –
   You'll be in that 'ere haw !
That feller do me so annoy;
   But he don't care a straw !

How goo the time ? I kind o' think
   Our fourses should be here.
Chaps, don't yow fare to want some drink ? –
   There's Sue with the old beer.
The rain have cleared right slap away,
   An' if it hold out bright,
Let's work right hard, lads (what d'ye say ?)
   An' clear this feld tonight !
John Lushington, A New Year's Budget, *(1866), pp. 11–12.*

The Harvest Horkey

The greatest festival for the men was the Harvest Home, or Horkey
which took place at each farmers after the last load had been safely
stacked. Everyone on the farm collected on the field where the last
sheaves remained, and shouts and cheers, went up as the wagon was
being filled. The last sheaf of all, generally a small one, was dressed
with green leaves and set on top of the waggon, which was followed
to the stack-yard by the procession of reapers, gleaners and onlookers
shouting 'holler largess' and collecting money from passers by. The
sheaf on the horkey load or the bough which was sometimes its
substitute, was by some fixed on their barn door, or on the gable end
of the roof. Some said it was for the bride, others for luck, but a wise

woman told me the corn was for Woden's horse, so that he should not kick holes in the thatch when he came in the Autumn.

The horkey feast followed. Only the men took part in it; plenty of good things were set before them, and a good deal of drinking, rough play and jokes went on. Some who could not walk home afterwards were sent home in wagons or wheeled in wheel-barrows, if near, and if there were not too many broken crowns or bones after the horkey feast, it was because their dumb beasts had had no share of their masters' beer, and took the way safely to their own stables where the women-folk fetched their men out of the straw into which they had fallen. . .

Emma Osmund, Survivals of Early Culture in Later Civilisation, *(1903- 4), pp. 11 & 14 : SRO (B) Acc. 788*

Gleaning Time in Suffolk

Why, listen yow – be quiet, bo'! –
    the bell is tolling eight ! –
Why don't yow mind what yow're about ? –
    We're allers kind o' late !
Now, Mary get that mawther dress'd –
    oh dear ! how slow you fare –
There come a lot o' gleaners now –
    Maw', don't stand gawkin' there !

Now, Jane, goo get that 'ere coach,
    an put the pillars in –
Oh ! won't I give it yow, my dear,
    if I do once begin !
Get that 'ere bottle, too –
ah, yow may well stand there an' sneer;
What will yowr father say, d'ye think,
    If we don't taak his beer ?

Come, Willie ! – Jane, where is he gone ?
    Goo yow an' fetch that child;
If yow don't move them legs of yow'rn,

yow'll make me kind o'riled !
There, lock the door, an' lay the key
      behind that 'ere old plate;
An' Jenny, yow run on afore,
      And ope the whatefield gate.

Well, here we be at last – oh dear !
      How fast my heart do beat !
Now, Jane, set yow by this 'ere coach,
an' don't yow leave yow'r seat,
Till that 'ere precious child's asleep;
      then bring yow that 'ere sack,
An' see if yow can't try to-day,
to kind o'bend yowr back !
Yow'll all wish, when the winter come,
      an yow ha'ent got no bread,
That for all drawlin' about so,
      yow'd harder wrought instead;
For all your father 'arn must goo
      old Skin 'ems rent to pay,
An' Mister Last, the shoemaker;
      so work yow hard I pray !

Dear me ! there goo the bell agin –
      'tis seven, I declare;
An' we don't 'pear to have got none: -
      the gleaning now don't fare
To be worth nothin'; but I think –
      as far as I can tell –
we'll try a comb, some how, to scratch,
          if we be 'live an' well.

John Lushington, A New Year's Budget, *(1866), pp. 13–14.*

Agriculture in 1873

Throughout the nineteenth century Ransome of Ipswich, Garrett of Leiston, Smyth of Peasenhall and Boby of Bury, were leading innovators and manufacturers of agricultural machinery.

The productions of the county are wheat, barley, peas, beans, seeds of various kinds, mangolds, turnips, and other roots. The wheat is of excellent quality, and usually commands a high price. The barley is amongst the best grown in England, and is largely malted for the Burton and other large breweries. Mangel wurtzel and turnips are grown of great weight and good quality for grazing purposes. Some farmers grow flax in the neighbourhood of Eye, Debenham, and Framlingham; and factories are in operation for preparing the flax. There is a great whole-sale trade in cattle, corn, malt, etc., at different markets in the county, especially Ipswich and Bury. Suffolk manufacturers are such as are in some way connected with agriculture.

There is no other part of England containing so many manufacturers of engines and machines for agricultural purposes, or where the implements of husbandry are made more perfect than in Suffolk... The principal firms are Messrs. Ransomes, Sims, and Head, Ipswich; Messrs Garrett and Sons, Leiston; Messrs E.R. and F. R. Turner, Ipswich; Messrs. Woods, Cocksedge, and Warner, Stowmarket; Mr. Burrell, Thetford. There are many other firms engaged in this department of industry; but as we are only drawing up a rapid sketch of the county, we must pass them by. We may be justified in assigning the foremost place among agricultural machinists to Messrs. Ransoms, Sims, and Head, and Messrs. Garrett. Both their concerns were of humble origin, and rose from small beginnings to colossal dimensions. Their engines and implements may be found in every English county, in every country in Europe, and in our Colonies.

The manufacture of artificial manure is also carried on to a great extent, especially from coprolites, which are found in great abundance in Suffolk. This branch of business was begun more than twenty years ago by Mr. E. Packard, of Saxmundham, on a very small scale, and the firm of which that gentleman is the head now sends out 20,000 tons annually of manure made from coprolites; while Messrs. Fison of

Ipswich, Messrs. Prentice, of Stowmarket, and other manufacturers, produce very large quantities of this and other kinds of artificial manures. Messrs. Prentice have also established the manufacture of gun cotton.

A. D. Bayne, The Royal Illustrated History of the Eastern Counties, (1873), vol. i, pp. 299-300.

Diversification in 1889

With present day farming bedevilled with Foot and Mouth, Swine Fever, quotas, severely reduced income and the renewed emphasis on diversification and farmer's markets, the discovery of this account was both apt and surprising.

At the bar of our inn [Rose and Crown, Sudbury] we met a burly farmer (of the genuine John Bull type, as personified in political cartoons) smoking his pipe and taking his ease, looking the very picture of prosperous contentment – for all the world as though wheat were many shillings a quarter dearer than it is, and the harvest prospects favourable instead of doubtful. 'Good morning, sir,' he said cheerily as we came in; 'fine weather for travelling.' We returned the greeting, adding that we hoped the weather was equally good for farming purposes, with some passing remark as to the depressed state of agriculture. 'Well, times are not over-brilliant,' he answered; 'but I don't complain. I manage to jog along comfortably enough.' Here was a surprise for us; we had actually come across a farmer who did not take the gloomy view of things. Perhaps, however we thought, he is the happy owner of the land he cultivates, and having consequently no rent to pay, he sees things in a different light from the man who has to meet, or endeavour to meet, his landlord's demands every half-year; but, after all, it turned out that we were wrong in our supposition. Our farmer was only a tenant like the majority, and paid a fair rent for 'good and useful land, but nothing wonderful.' From what we could gather in the course of our conversation, instead of struggling against the inevitable, he acknowledged the changed condition of affairs brought on by foreign competition, and no longer stuck abjectly to the old rotation of crops because they paid for the growing thus in the times of protection. From what we could make out, the secret of his comparative prosperity appeared to be in always, where possible, securing two profits upon his productions: he did not sell his raw material to others who take the lion's share of the profit; he converted his corn into pork, beef and mutton; he did not sell his milk or cream, but converted them into cheese and butter; he made his fruit into jam. He ground his own corn, and secured for himself the miller's profit; so with careful management, doing away as far as possible with the middleman, our farmer managed, in spite of these latter evil days, to put a good face to the world, and to live comfortably, though fortune-making was out of the question. I doubt much, however, in spite of his enterprise, whether he could 'put anything by for a rainy day.'

One unexpected result of the agricultural depression – a result that may be a gain to some – is that sundry farmers, at their wit's end how to pay their rent, have discovered a new source of revenue by the letting of apartments with board, or even a portion of their farmhouse, to families when leaving town for their usual summer outing, and, having tried the experiment with profit, are repeating it. And a very welcome change from the usual run of seaside lodgings is the roomy and picturesque farmhouse, with the green fields for the children to romp and play in, the country around to explore, the farming operations to watch, the gathering of the crops, the outgoing and the incoming of the teams, the milking of the cows, the feeding of the live stock, and perchance the haymaking to help with, not forgetting the plentiful supply of fresh-laid eggs, milk, and vegetables, all to be had at the market price . . . Perhaps I may here state that I have with myself and family (much to our enjoyment and the health of the little ones) stayed at farmhouse apartments, so I write having some experience in the matter. On one occasion our stay was for eight weeks, and on another for six, and friends of mine have also tried the same experiment, and the results in each case has been an unqualified success. At one farmhouse where I was, the tenant confessed to me that he found by letting apartments one year he received the full amount of his rent; he owned that neither himself or his wife liked the idea at all at first, but he had been fortunate in always having pleasant people, and now he rather enjoyed the change of having visitors – they interested him. Thus out of evil some good may come.

James Hissey, A Tour in a Phaeton, (1889), pp. 323–26.

Tractors and Horses

George Garrard who had a six-horse farm at Gislingham bought his first tractor in 1927: 'I had an Emerson-Brantigan, a big owd thing that drew a three-furrow plough. There were only about half a dozen of them in the county.' When he bought the tractor he sold two of his horses, working his land with four horses and the tractor. Later, he bought another tractor – a Standard Fordson, and sold another two horses. He kept two tractors and two horses right up to the 1939–45 war when, to a certain extent, the farm-horse came into his own again.

This is what happened to George Garrard's farm: 'During the war one of my tractors broke down and it was difficult to get spare parts. So I say: 'I got two tractors and one is no good, so I am going to get some good horses'. I went to a sale . . . there were two Suffolks – one forty-five guineas and one forty-two – a gelding and a mare. They say the mare was two year old and had now been at work a-carting beet. I say: 'I want something that can work,' so I bought the mare. I took her hoom and soon found she was a right good worker. But one day one of the men say to me, he say: 'Thet mare is in foal'. 'No!' I say. But he were right. I kept her in the yard and on light work; and one morning I went into the yard; and there was a beautiful little foal. The man I bought her from wanted to buy the mare and foal back for a hundred guineas; but I wouldn't part with them. And a little later I bought another colt to run in with mine.

For a long time I worked the horses along with the tractors: I used the horses for ploughing the headlands after the tractors had ploughed the stetches; and for finishing-up, as we called it. We used to plough the last two furrows in the stetch with the horses so that the tractor-wheel wouldn't go on land that had already been ploughed. In the heavy owd land where I was, the tractor wheels can very easy form a hard pan – a hard layer of mud that you wouldn't be able to break up till the following winter. I sold the colts; and then I sold the two horses in 1953 – they went to the knackers. They bought in sixty guineas each, much more than I paid for 'em.'

As this account indicates the tractor gained ground very quickly after the last war; and during the early 'fifties the tractor-plough ousted the horse-plough from most of the farms in Suffolk.

George Ewart Evans, The Horse in the Furrow, (1960), pp. 156-57.

3 · MEDIEVAL AND TUDOR

The Martyrdom of Edmund, King of East Anglia : 869

Then the holy King Eadmund was taken in his palace [at Hegelisdun] as a member of Christ, his weapons thrown aside, and was pinioned and tightly bound with chains . . . And so in chains he was mocked in many ways, and at length, after being savagely beaten, he was brought to a tree in the neighbourhood, tied to it, and for a long while tortured with terrible lashes. But his constancy was unbroken, while without ceasing he called on Christ with broken voice. This roused the fury of his enemies, who, as if practising at a target, pierced his whole body with arrow-spikes, augmenting the severity of his torment by frequent discharges of their weapons, and inflicting wound upon wound, while one javelin made room or another. And thus, all haggled over by the sharp points of their darts, and scarce able to draw breath, he actually bristled with them, like a prickly hedgehog or thistle fretted with spines, resembling in his agony the illustrious martyr Sebastian . . .

Thus while the words of prayer were still on his lips, the executioner, sword in hand, deprived the king of life, striking off his head with a single blow. The sacred head which had been anointed not with oil of sinners, but with the sacramental chrism of mystery, was carried by them as they retired into a wood, the name of which is Haglesdun, and was thrown as far as possible among the dense thickets of brambles, and so hidden . . .

The head of the holy king, far removed from the body to which it belonged, broke into utterance without assistance from the vocal chords, or aid from the arteries proceeding from the heart. A number of the party, like corpse-searchers, were gradually examining the out-of-the-way parts of the wood, and when the moment had arrived at which the sound of the voice could be heard, the head, in response to the calls of the search-party mutually encouraging one another, and as comrade to comrade crying alternately 'Where are you ?' indicated the place where it lay by exclaiming in their native tongue, Here! Here! Here! In Latin the same meaning would be rendered by Hic! Hic! Hic! And the head never ceased to repeat this exclamation, till all were drawn to it... And to this miracle the Creator of the world added another by attaching an unwonted guardian to the heavenly treasure. In fact, a monstrous wolf was by God's mercy found in that place, embracing the holy head between its paws, as it lay at full length on the ground, and thus acting as sentinel to the martyr. Nor did it suffer any animal whatever to injure its charge, but, forgetful of its natural voracity, preserved the head from all harm with the utmost vigilance, lying outstretched on the earth . . . and never afterwards was there seen in that neighbourhood any wolf so terrible in appearance. When the wolf had retired, those who were intrusted with the duty, with the utmost care and with all possible zeal and skill provisionally fitted the head to the sacred body, and committed the two joined together to a becoming sepulchre. And there they built over the grave a chapel of rude construction, in which the body rested for many years.

And so, when a seasonable opportunity was found [c.903] they displayed in many ways the devotion which they cherished in regard to the blessed king and martyr Edmund. They were stirred by occurrence of marvellous works. For the Saint, from beneath the lowly roof of his consecrated abode, made manifest by frequent miraculous signs the magnitude of his merits in the sight of God. These events aroused great numbers of the inhabitants of that province, high and low alike; and in the royal town which, in the English tongue, is called Bedrices-gueord, but in Latin is called Bedrici-curtis, they erected a church of immense size, with storeys admirably constructed of wood, and to this they translated him with great magnificence, as was due . . .

And so the king and martyr Eadmund was with reverence pronounced to be a Saint . . .

(Archdeacon Herman, writing c. 1095 believed Edmund was 'entombed, as are certified by the tradition of our elders, in a little village called Sutton, close to the scene of his martyrdom.' Both Hegilsdun and Sutton are in the parish of Bradfield St. Clare.)

Abbo of Fleury. 'The Passion of St. Edmund', c.985, in Lord Francis Hervey (ed) The Garland of St. Edmund King and Martyr, (1907), pp.33–45

Hoxne Market and Eye Castle

At Hoxne, the site of the market is a small wedge-shaped green at the heart of the 'village', to the south of the large medieval church of SS. Peter and Paul, and to the east of the Anglo-Saxon bishop's manor-house . . . The sad story of that market is told in Domesday Book:

> In this manor there used to be a market, and it continued after King William came. And it was a Saturday market. And William Malet made his castle at Eye. And on the same day as the market used to be held on the Bishop's manor at Hoxne, William Malet established another market at the castle at Eye. And thereby the Bishop's market has been so far spoilt that it is of little worth; and now it is set up on Fridays. But the market at Eye is held on the Saturday.

Saturday was obviously a better market-day than Friday in the 1080s, as it is still in the 1970s. William Malet died in 1071 in the campaign in the Fens against Hereward. So we have a date for the creation of the town of Eye, in the precise form we see today, it was all laid out, and built, on its island (which is what its name means) between 1066 and 1071, just nine centuries ago. The island is formed by the broad meadows of the Dove on the east, the stream from Yaxley to the north, and the 'Town Moor', a lovely willowy common, very 'Dutch' looking, across the south-west-side. This 'moor' may be partly artificial, like Framlingham's great 'Mere', on the north side of the Bigod castle. They would be produced as part of the defensive 'moating', in the course of quarrying thousands of loads of earth to create the steep motte on which the 'Keep' of the castle stood.

Norman Scarfe, The Suffolk Landscape, (1972), pp. 151-52 (and 2002).

The Battle of Fornham : 1173

In October 1173, the forces of Henry II gathered at Bury, to intercept the Earl of Leicester and his mercenary Fleming army, who were intent on replacing Henry with his son. Hugh Bigod, the Earl of Norfolk and Suffolk, provided the rebel power base at Framlingham and Bungay, but was not present on this, the only medieval battle-field in Suffolk.

Robert de Lucy, Lord Chief Justice of England, who was repelling an invasion of the Scots, hastened to Bury. His army included 300 knights, with the forces of the district hastily gathered together under one of the sheriffs, and possibly some armed servants of the Abbey. With him were Humphrey de Bohun, High Constable and the Earls of Cornwall, Gloucester and Arundel. The entire array numbered perhaps, 1,500. With the sacred banner of St. Edmund at their head they marched out of Bury by the North and Risby gates, and united their forces at the bridge formerly known as 'Cossie' (evidently causeway) at Fornham . . .

Leicester found that rain had made the ford impassable, and addressing Hugh de Castele said: 'We will accept battle, very hard and heavy though it be. Behold the hauberks and helmets shining against the sun. Be knights, for God's sake, I command you, and woe to the body of the man who first runs away. Let it never be said as a proverb that we were recreants. His troops included 3,000 Flemings, in whom he placed great confidence, 40 knights and their attendants, and some archers . . .

He drew up his army in the Fornham meadows, facing Bury, with the swollen river guarding its right flank.

Walter Fitz Robert made a furious charge upon them, but was repulsed, and on rejoining the main body urged the Earl of Arundel to advance, otherwise their enemies would destroy them. Humphrey de Bohun then charged and took over 100 prisoners. The whole line of the Royal Army attacked, and the Flemings were broken and scattered. They seem to have still fought bravely, and Leicester tried to rally them. His wife attempted to escape, but was thrown into a ditch, and in extricating herself lost her rings . . .

Leicester seems to have made his last stand near where the ruins of the church of St. Genevieve stand in the park. He now surrendered, and with the countess and other prisoners was subsequently sent into Normandy and placed in confinement in Falaisi.

H. Barker, 'The Battle of Fornham', The Bury and Norwich Post, *13 May 1921*.

Abbot Sampson examines the Body of St. Edmund: 1198

And the Abbot said that it was his great desire to behold his patron and that he wished that the Sacrist and Walter the physician would go with him to look upon the body; and there were nominated two chaplains of the Abbot and two guardians of the feretory and two masters of the vestry, and another six: Hugh the Sacrist, Walter the physician, Augustine, William of Diss, Robert and Richard. So, while the Convent slept, these twelve put on albs and, drawing forth the coffin from the feretory, they carried it and, setting it on a table near the ancient place of the feretory, they made ready to remove the lid, which was attached and fastened to the coffin by sixteen very long nails. And when they had done this with difficulty, they were all bidden to retire to a distance saving the Abbot's two associates whom I named above. And the coffin was so filled with the holy body, both lengthways and across, that a needle could scarce be placed between the Saint's head or feet and the wood; and the head lay united to the body, and raised a little on a small pillow. The Abbot, therefore, standing close by, looked within and found first a silken cloth veiling the whole body, and after that a linen cloth of wondrous whiteness: and over the head was a small linen cloth and beneath it a small cloth of silk, finely woven, like a nun's veil. And afterwards they found the body wrapped in a linen cloth, and then at last the lineaments of the holy body were revealed. Here the Abbot stopped, saying that he did not dare go further, to see the sacred flesh unclothed. Therefore taking the head between his hands, he said groaning, 'Glorious Martyr, Saint Edmund, blessed be the hour when thou wast born! Glorious Martyr, turn not to my perdition this my boldness, that I, a miserable sinner, now touch thee; thou knowest my devotion, thou knowest my intent.' And he proceeded to touch the eyes and the nose, which was very large and prominent, and after he touched the breast and arms and, raising the left hand, he touched the fingers and placed his fingers between the fingers of the saint; and going further he found the feet turned stiffly upwards as of a man dead that self-same day, and he touched the toes of the feet and counted them as he touched them . . .

H.E.Butler (ed), The Chronicle of Jocelin of Brakelond, (1949), pp.113-114.

The Head of Simon of Sudbury

Simon of Sudbury was Chancellor of England, Archbishop of Canterbury and the man who introduced the Poll Tax – for which he was beheaded by the mob at the Tower of London. His is the best preserved medieval head in England.

We were taken at once to the vestry [*of St Gregory's Church, Sudbury*], and, opening a little cupboard in the wall, there the clerk showed us the shrivelled head of the Archbishop – and a gruesome sight it was, with the ears and skin upon it dried up like parchment, looking even more ghastly than that of an Egyptian mummy. The head had been recently varnished by a local doctor, so we were informed the better to preserve it. Below it, in puzzling old English letters, is the following inscription:-

> The Head of Simon Theobald who was born at Sudbury and
> thence called Simon of Sudbury. He was sent when but a
> Youth into fforeign Parts to study the Civil Law. Whereof he
> was made Doctor. He visited most of the Universities of ffrans.
> was made Chaplain to pope Innocent and Auditor Rota,
> a Judge of thee Roman Court. By interest of this Pope
> he was made Chancellor of Salisbury. In the Year 1361 he
> was consecrated Bishop of London, and in the year 1375 was
> translated to the See of Canterbury and made Chancellor of
> England. While he was Bishop of London he Built the
> upper part of St. Gregory's in Sudbury : and where his
> ffather's House Stood he erected a College of Secular Priests
> and endowed it with the Yearly Revenue of one Hundred
> Twenty-two pounds eighteen shillings, and was at length
> barbarously Beheaded on Tower Hill in London by the
> Rabble in Wat Tyler's Rebellion in the Reign of
> Richard 2d 1381.

The body of the unfortunate Archbishop lies beneath an altar-tomb in Canterbury Cathedral. It seemed to us a pity that his head is not allowed to rest in peace there also, instead of being made a sort of vulgar peepshow of, to gratify idle curiosity. The day for relics has gone by.

James Hissey. A Tour in a Phaeton, (1889) pp. 327-329.

The Devil's Gift.

It fortuned that in a market town in the county of Suffolk there was a stage play, in the which play one called John Adroyns – which lived in another village 2 miles from this – played the devil. And when the play was done, this John Adroyns, in the evening, departed from the said market town to go home to his own house; and because he had with him no change of clothing, he went forth in his devil's apparel. In the way coming homeward, he came through a warren of conies [rabbits] belonging to a gentleman of the village where he himself dwelt.

At which time it fortuned that a priest, a vicar of a church thereby, with two or three other unthrifty fellows, had brought with them a horse, a net and a fetter to the intent there to get conies. And when the ferret was in the earth and the net set over the pathway wherein this John Adroyns should come, this priest and these other fellows saw him come – in the devil's raiment! Considering that they themselves were in the devil's service and stealing conies, and supposing that here came the devil indeed, they for fear ran away. This John Adroyns, in the devil's raiment and because it was somewhat dark, saw not the net but went forth in haste and stumbled thereat and fell down and with the fall had almost broke his neck.

But when he was a little revived, he looked up and spied it was a net to catch conies, and looked further and saw that they ran away for fear of him, and saw tied to a bush a horse laden with conies which they had taken. And he took the horse and net and leapt upon the horse, and rode to the gentleman's place that was lord of the warren, to the intent to have his thanks for taking such a prey. And when he came, knocked at the gates. To whom, anon, one of the gentlemen's servants asked who was there, and suddenly opened the gate: and as soon as he perceived him in the devil's raiment was suddenly abashed, and sparred the door again and went in to his master and said – and sware to his master – that the devil was at the gate and would come in.

The gentleman, hearing him say so, called the steward of his house, the wisest servant that he had, and bade him go to the gate and bring him sure word who was there. The steward thought he would see surely who was there, came to the gate and looked through the chinks in divers places, and saw well that it was the devil, sat upon a horse, and saw hanging about the saddle on every side the coney-heads hanging down. Then he came to his master, afeard, in great haste, and said: 'By God's body, it is the devil indeed that's at the gate, sitting upon a horse laden with souls; and by likelihood, he is come for your soul purposely, and lacketh but your soul; and if he had your soul, I suppose he should be gone.'

This gentlemen, then marvellously abashed, called upon his chaplain, and made the holy candle to be lit, and gat holy waters, and went to the gate with as many of his servants as durst go with him, where the holy chaplain, with holy words of conjuration, said: 'In the name of the fader, son and holy ghost, I conjure thee and charge thee in the holy name of god to tell my why and wherfore thou comest hither.'

This John Adroyns (in the devil's apparel), hearing them begin to conjure in such a manner, said: 'Nay, nay, be not afeared of me, for I am a good devil. I am John Adroyns, your neighbour dwelling in this village, and he that played the devil today in the play. I have brought my master a dozen or two of his own conies that were stolen in his warren, and the thieves' horse and their net, and made them for to run away.

And when they heard him thus speak, by his voice they knew him well enough and opened the gate and let him come in. And so all the aforesaid fear and dread was turned to mirth and disport.

MORAL: By this tale ye may see that men fear many times more than they need. Which hath caused men to believe that spirits and devils have been seen in divers places, when it hath been nothing so.

'A Hundred Merry Tales, 1526', Suffolk in the Middle Ages, Norman Scarfe, (1986), pp. 167-68.

The Hair of Mary Tudor, Queen of France.

Mary Tudor, the sister of Henry VIII, wife of Louis XII of France and then in 1515, wife of Charles Brandon, Duke of Suffolk. Their main residence was Westhorpe Hall, where Mary died in 1533. She was buried in Bury Abbey and, on its closure in 1539, her body was moved to St. Mary's Church.

The corpse of the sister of Henry VIII was subjected to a second disinterment. Room was wanted for the communicants at St. Mary's altar in 1784, when the tomb was pulled down. Everyone supposed it was a mere cenotaph, but the queen's body was discovered, within the space formed by the stone slabs, lapt in a leaden case somewhat resembling the human form. On the breast was engraved, 'Marye, Quene of Ffranc, 1533, Edmund B.' the body was in a wonderful state of preservation, a profusion of long fair hair glittering like gold was spread over it; of this a handful was cut off by Sir John Cullum. Several of the antiquaries present at the exhumation of the Queen-duchess likewise possessed themselves of part of this abundant chevelure, which had resisted all the deforming powers of corruption. Little did Mary, the lovely Queen-duchess, and her attendant maidens think, when these far-famed tresses of paly gold were combed out and braided at her bridal toilet with pride and care, that a day would come when they would be profaned by the rude grasp of strange men, and even subjected to the hammer of an auctioneer.

In the beginning of the present century, a lock of this queen's hair was advertised, lotted, and puffed in the catalogue of the household furniture of a deceased Beccles antiquary, who had taken it from her tomb: aye, and it was knocked down to the best bidder, in company with chairs and tables, pots, spits, kettles, and pans.

Agnes Strickland, Lives of the Tudor Princesses, *(1868), pp. 92–93.*

The Tempest and Black Dog
at Blythbury and Bungay : 1577

TEMPEST IN SUFFOLK On Sundaie the fourth of August, between the hours of nine and ten of the clocke in the forenoone, whilst the Minister was reading of the second lesson in the Parish Churche of

Bliborough, a Towne in Suffolk, a strange and Terrible Tempest of Lightning and Thunder strake through the wall of the same churche into the ground, almost a yard deepe, drave downe all the people on that side above twentie persons, then renting the wall up to the Vestrie, clefte the doore, and returning to the Steeple, rent the timber, brake the Chimes, and fled towards BONGAIE, a Towne six miles off. The people that were stricken downe were found grovelling more than halfe an houre after, whereof, one man more than fortie yeares, and a boie of fifteene yeares old were found starke dead: the others were scorched. The same, or like flash of Lightning and cracks of Thunder rent the Parish Church of BONGIE, nine miles from Norwich, wroong insunder the wiers and wheels of the Clocke, singd two men which sat in the Belfreie, when the others were at procession or suffrages, and scorched another, which hardlie escaped.

Immediately herrupon, there appeared in a most horrible similitude and likenesse to the congregation, then and there present, A DOG as they might discerne it, of a BLACK COLOUR; at the sight whereof, together with the fearful flashes of fire then were seene, moved such admiration in the minds of the assemblie, that they thought doomes day was already come.

THIS BLACK DOG, or the Divel in such a likenesse (God hee knoweth all who worketh all) running all along down the body of the Church with great swiftnesse, and incredible haste, among the people, in a visible forme and shape, passed between two persons, as they were kneeling on their knees, and occupied in prayer as it seemed, wrung the necks of them bothe at one instant, clene backward, insomuche that even in a moment where they kneeled they stra'gely dyed.

This is a wonderful example of God's wrath, no doubt to terrifie us, that wee might feare him for his justice, or putting back our footsteps from the pathes of sinne, to love him for his mercy.

To our matter again. There was at ye same time another wunder wrought: for the same BLACK DOG, still continuing and remaining in one and the self-same shape, passing by an other man of the congregation in the Chuurch, gave him such a gripe in the back, that therewith all he was presently drawen together and shrunk up, as it were a piece of lether scorched in a hot fire; or at the mouth of a purse or bag. drawen together with a string; the man, albeit he was in so straunge a taking, dyed not, but, as it is thought, is yet alive: which thing is marvellous in the eyes of men, and offereth muche matter of amasing the minde.

BUNGAY BURIAL REGISTER

'1577. John Fuller and Adam Walker slayne in the tempest, in the belfry, in the tyme of prayer, upon the Lord's day, ye iiiith of August.'

Tract of 1577 reprinted in A. Suckling, History and Antiquities of the County of Suffolk, *(1846), vol i, pp. 124-26*

Queen Elizabeth's Progress : 1578

Queen Elizabeth made a flying visit to Suffolk in August 1578, in order to enforce religious conformity amongst the gentry. Protestants and conforming Catholics were honoured with visits and rewards, while recusant Catholics were arrested and imprisoned. One such was Edward Rookwood of Euston whose relative Ambrose Rookwood of Coldham Hall, Stanningfield, was later to be executed with Guy Fawkes for his part in the Gunpowder Plot.

They [the people of Suffolk and Norfolk] hadde but small warning certaynely to build upon, of the comming of the Queenes Majestie into both these sheeres, the gentlemen had made such ready provision, that all the velvets and the silkes were taken up that might be layde hand on, and bought for any money, and soone converted to such garments and sutes of roabes, that the shew thereof might have beautifyed the greatest triumph that was in Englande these many years.

For, as I hearde, there were, two hundred young gentlemen, clad in white velvet, and three hundred of the graver sorte, apparelled in black velvet coates,and fair chaynes, all ready at one instant and place, with fifteen hundred servingmen more, on horseback, well and bravely mounted, in good order, ready to receive the Queen's Highness into Suffolk, which surely was a comely troope, and a noble sight to behold. And all these waited on the sheriff, Sir William Spring, during the Queen's majesties abode in these parties, and to the very confines of Suffolk; but, before her Highness passed into Norfolk, there was in Suffolke such sumptuous feasting and bankets as seldom in any part of the world hath been seen before. The Maister of the Rolls, Sir William Cordell, of Long Melford Hall, was one of the firste that begaine this great feasting and did light such a candle to the rest of the shire that many were glad bountifully and frankly to follow the same example, with such charge and costs, as the whole traine were in some sorte pleased therewith. And neare Bury, Sir William Drury, of Hawstead, for his part, at his house, made the Queen's Highnesse a costly and delicat dinner; and Sir Robert Jermyn of Roshbroke feasted the French embassadoures two several times; with which charges and courtesie they stood marvellously contented. The sheriffe, Sir William Spring, Sir Thomas Kytson, Sir Arthur Higham, and divers others of worship, kept great houses, and sundry, either at the Queen's coming or return, solemnly feasted her Highness, yea, and defrayed the whole charges, for a day or twayne; presented gifts, made such triumphs and devices, as indede was most noble to beholde, and very thankfully accepted . . .

[*The Queen stayed with Sir Thomas Barnardiston at Keddington and George Colt at Cavendish on the 1st and 2nd August; with Sir William Cordell at Long Melford on the 3rd and 4th August; She had lunch with Henry Drury at Lawshall, and supper with Sir William Drury at Hawstead on 5th August; was at Bury on the 6th; at Euston with Edward Rookwood on the 7th August. She then went into Norfolk and visited Kenninghall, Norwich, Woodrising and Thetford. From 28th – 30th August she stayed at Hengrave Hall*].

. . . Sir Thomas Kytson's, where in very deede the fare and banquet did so exceed a number of other places that it is worthy the mention. A show representing the fayries, as well as might be, was there seene; in the which show a riche jewell was presented to the Queen's Highness.

Thomas Churchyard, 'The Entertaynmente of the Queenes Majestie into Suffolke and Norffolke', John Nicols, The Progresses of Queen Elizabeth, (1788), vol. ii, pp. 51-54.

Orford Castle

Orford castle was built 1165 – 73, and was the first English castle to have a circular faceted keep with towers. A drawing of 1601 shows the beacon to be on top of the keep.

BEACON for barks that navigate the stream
Of Ore, or Alde, or breast old Ocean's spray;
Land-mark for inland travellers—far away
O'er heath and sheep-walk—as bright morning's beam,
Or evening sunset's richer, mellow gleam
Lights up thy weather-beaten turrets grey;
Still dost thou bear thee bravely in decay,
As if thy by-gone glories were no dream!
E'en now with lingering grandeur thou look'st down
From thy once fortified, embattled hill,
Striving thine ancient office to fulfil;
And though thy keep be now the only crown
Of Orford's desolate and dwindled town,
Seem'st to assert thyself its sovereign still.
Bernard Barton, Household Verses, *(1845) p.226*

4 · TOWNS AND VILLAGES

Bury St Edmunds in 1698

So to St. Edmunds-Bury 8 mile – but as had often been observed before the miles are very long – I pass'd by two or 3 little villages and about two miles off there is the town of St. Edmunds Bury which appears standing on a great hill; the towers and buildings look so compact and well together with the trees and gardens thick about it the prospect was wonderfully pleasant; its but two parishes; the Market Cross has a dyal and lanthorn on the top, and there being another house close to it high built with such a tower and lanthorn also, with the two churches towers and some other buildings pretty good made it appear nobly at a distance; this high house [Cupola House] is an apothecarys, at least 60 stepps up from the ground and gives a pleaseing prospect of the whole town, that is compact severall streetes but no good buildings; except this the rest are great old houses of timber and mostly in the old forme of the country which are long peaked roofes of tileing; this house is the new mode of building, 4 roomes of a floore pretty sizeable and high, well furnish'd . . .

There was two streets were broad and very long out of which run a cross 5 or 6 streets more, which are as good in most country towns, they were well pitch'd with small stones; there are many Descenters in the town 4 Meeteing places with the Quakers and Anabaptists, there is only the ruines of the Abby walls and the fine gate at the entrance that remaines stone well carv'd; it seems to be a thriveing industrious town 4 gates in it.

There are a great deale of gentry which lives in the town tho' there are no good houses but what are old rambling ones, they are in what they call the Green a space by the churches [St. Mary's and St. James'] it's a very dear place so much Company living in the town makes provision scarce and dear, however it's a good excuse to raise the reckoning on strangers.

Christopher Morris (ed), The Journeys of Celia Fiennes, *1698, (1949), pp. 151-52.*

Ipswich in 1722

The country around Ipswich, as are all the counties so near the coast, is applied chiefly to corn, of which a very great quantity is continually shipped off for London, and sometimes they load the corn here for Holland, especially if the market abroad is encouraging. They have 12 parish churches in this town with three or four meeting houses, but there are not so many Quakers here as at Colchester, and no Anabaptists, or anti-poedo Baptists, that I could hear of, at least there is no meeting house of that denomination. There is one meeting house for the Presbyterians, one for the Independents and one for the Quakers. The first is as large and fine a building of that kind as most on this side of England, and the inside the best finished of any I have seen, London not excepted; that for the Independents is a handsome new-built building, but not so gay or so large as the other.

There is a great deal of very good company in this town, and though there are not so many of the gentry here as at Bury, yet there are more here than in any other town in the county, and I observed particularly that the company you meet with here are generally persons well informed of the world and who have something very solid and entertaining in their society. I take this town to be one of the most agreeable places in England, for families who have lived well but may have suffered in our late calamities of stocks and bubbles, to retreat to, where they may live within their own compass, and several things indeed recommend it to such: 1. Good houses at easy rents. 2. An airy, clean and well governed town. 3. very Agreeable and improving company almost of very kind. 4. A wonderful plenty of all manner of provisions, whether flesh or fish, and very good of the mind. 5. Those provisions very cheap, so that a family may live here cheaper than in any town in England of its bigness, within such a small distance from London. 6. Easy passage to London, either by land or water, the coach going through to London in a day.

The Lord Viscount Hereford has a very fine seat and park in this town; the house indeed is old-built, but very commodious. It is called Christchurch, having been as it is said, a priory, or religious in former times. The green and park is a great addition to the pleasures of this town, the inhabitants being allowed to divert themselves there with walking, bowling, etc.

Daniel Defoe, A Tour Thro' the Whole Island of Great Britain, (1724), pp. 45-46.

Newmarket in 1724

Newmarket stands in a plain, that has a Prospect three quarters of the Compass. It consists of two Parishes, one in Suffolk, one in Cambridgeshire; but their Market-place and whole Street is in the former, which occasions those that live on the South side, says our Author, to hang all their Sign-Posts on Hinges, so that when the Fancy takes them they may draw them to the Sides of the Wall, and consequently into their own County. They have a Market on Tuesdays, well supplied with Fish, Wild Fowl, Pigeons, &c. and the Women have some spinning White-Work here; tho' the Growth of the Town is not owing to any Manufacture or particular Commodity, but to the Conveniency of Passengers, and the Advantage of the Court which has often been drawn hither for the Diversions of Hunting and Horse-Racing; and there is a House built on purpose for the Reception of our Kings on Cambridge side. The Devil's Dyke runs all along New-Market Heath.

Herman Moll, A New Description of England and Wales, (1724), p. 145.

In Praise of Bury St. Edmunds : 1825

To conclude an account of Suffolk and not to sing the praises of Bury St. Edmund's would offend every creature of Suffolk birth; even at Ipswich, when I was praising that place, the very people of that town asked me if I did not think Bury St. Edmund's the nicest town in the world. Meet them wherever you will, they have all the same boast; and indeed, as a town in itself, it is the neatest place that ever was seen. It is airy, it has several fine open places in it, and it has the remains of the famous abbey walls and the abbey gate entire; and it is so clean and so neat that nothing can equal it in that respect.
William Cobbett, Rural Rides, *Everyman Edition, (1914), p. 227.*

Ipswich in 1894

The immediate impression one receives, after a few hours stay in the busy, thriving little town, is that it has 'progress' written over it from end to end.

Look at the crowds passing up and down Tavern Street. Keen-faced mechanics, laughing, noisy factory girls, jovial farmers, prosperous manufacturers, and smartly-dresses women pass in an incessant stream, representing the interests of the town. Everybody seems busy, and there is always plenty to do. They have everything they need, provided by an excellent municipality.

East Anglians are certainly not 'slow going' in Ipswich, which has a magnificent Free Library, an Art Gallery, voluntary schools, smart newspapers, a race-course, Mechanic's Institute, recreation grounds, schools of science, and, as a well-meaning person, who was decanting on the advantages of the town, remarked, 'a cemetery which is laid out as tastefully as a gentleman's park.' Its great aim, apparently, is to be like London. Ipswich folk strive desperately hard to be lively and 'up to date,' and they succeed admirably. They have their fashionable quarter near the Lower Arboretum, where wealth and culture are very much in evidence; they have a couple of good theatres, they go out a great deal in the evenings, they are nothing if not artistic, and they have a miniature St. James's Hall, which seats some two thousand persons, and to which the best musical talent is invited.

As a manufacturing centre it can hold its own against much vaster towns, though its products are chiefly confined to agricultural implements. To almost every small householder in England the name of Ransomes, Sims, and Jefferies is familiar; but lawn-mowers and knife-machines are only the trifles produced by this huge Ipswich firm, whose works cover eleven acres and give employment to eighteen hundred men. Here one may study the progress of modern farming in the wonderful machines turned out by thousands from this famous manufactory. Steam ploughs, combined reapers, binders and threshers are exported hence to all parts of the world, helping to spread the fame of Ipswich as the home of agricultural science. There are all manner of other manufactories in the town, too, chiefly of chemical manures and stationery wares; but ladies corsets come in a good second to the agricultural machines; some two or three thousand men, boys, and girls, finding this industry the mainstay, so to say, of their existence . . .

People certainly make the best of everything at their command in this enterprising old town. They are fortunate in the possession of a charming river, but they are not merely content to let it run its course as best it may by their shores. With its new dock-gates, its improved river-bed, and its extended Quay at Ipswich, the Orwell has become quite an important river, with no inconsiderable steamship trade; and as one looks up the stream at the effective picture in which the shipping is so important a feature, it is easy to see that the craft lying at anchor in the dock are not mere pleasure boats and smart yachts and smacks. There are real vessels here of some two thousand tonnage, manned by real swarthy sailors who lend additional picturesqueness to the river-side that is here delightfully free from the usual riparian squalor. Huge machines and chemicals and much corn speed away down the bright and beautiful Orwell, which is now considerably more than ornamental to this district of East Anglia.

Mrs. Alfred Perlyn, Sunrise Land: Rambles in Eastern England, (1894), pp.150-1 & 157.

Dunwich

Dunwich was the ancient capital and See of the Bishop of East Anglia. It contained 8 parish churches, 3 religious houses and 2 hospitals. Storms between 1286 and 1330 destroyed the harbour and much of the town, and by 1400 the population had fallen to 800. Until 1832 the 'Town' still sent two M.P.s to Parliament. Nature's work of destruction continues today.

Where the lone cliff uprears its rugged head,
Where frowns the ruin o'er the silent dead.
Where creeps the billow on the lonely shore,
Where once the mighty lived, but live no more;
Where proudly frown'd the Convent's mossy wall,
Where rose the gothic tower, the stately hall,
Where bards proclaimed and warriors shared the feast,
Where ruled the baron, and where knelt the priest –
There stood the city in its pride – 'tis gone !
Mocked at by crumbling pile, and mouldering stone,
And shapeless masses which the reckless power
Of time hath hurled from arch and tower;
O'er the lone spot, where shrines and pillared halls
Once gorgeous shone, the clammy lizard crawls;
O'er the lone spot, where yawned the guarded fosse,
Creeps the wild bramble, and the spreading moss:
Oh ! time hath bowed that lordly city's brow,
In which the mighty dwelt – where dwell they now ?
James Bird, Dunwich, *(1828), pp. 1-2.*

Northgate: Beccles

I live in a medieval street in a small country town nine miles from the North Sea. Behind me is a pastoral landscape such as Constable painted. In front of me lives Fred. Fred plays in the water polo team; he is also a butcher. Next to Fred lives Sir Alexander in an eighteenth-century mansion. Next to Sir Alexander lives a man who drives a machine that resurfaces roads.

Next door on my side of the street lives an architect's widow who keeps bees. Next to her is The Anchor. Next to The Anchor is a boat-yard; opposite the boat-yard an ice-cream shop, next to the ice-cream shop lives a general—and so on. It would be difficult to find a more varied population in any street than there is in ours.

This street represents three revolutions in transport. First, it was a street of fishermen. They prayed to St. Peter. Before the parish church was built, even before William the Conqueror landed in England, fishermen used to pray to St. Peter in a chapel at the water's edge. The water in those days was salt; the fertile valley I see from my back windows was a sea estuary. Herrings were landed near St. Peter's chapel and brought up the sloping track called 'the Score' to the Old market, which was the fish market. And when the town wanted to be granted a charter, it had to pay 50,000 herrings for it. There used to be many inns in this street. One of the most popular was named The Coffin. To drink in The Coffin somehow rendered a seaman less likely to drowning, according to the mysterious contrary logic of their superstitions.

The estuary was drained long ago. Water still passes the Score, but it is now an embanked and controlled river. Before there were good roads, a river was the best thoroughfare. So the town's river-side became an industrial area. There was a quay, a tannery, a coal-yard, numerous maltings, a rope-maker's and builder of barges, or wherries as they are called. At least a hundred men, who drank a gallon of beer each before breakfast, worked as stevedores, tanners, maltsters, and wherrymen . . .

Then the railway came to town. The river fell out of use for the carriage of goods. The maltings have been converted into houses, and their yards and wharves into beautiful gardens. The quay is now a mooring-place of pleasure boats. And now, in process of time, the railway is in decline. Traffic, having once moved from the river across to the railway, has now moved back again towards the river; not quite as far as the river, but to this street which runs parallel to it. This narrow old street, only twelve feet wide in places, is choked all day with articulated lorries trying to pass timber drays, buses trying to get by the brewer's lorry as it unloads barrels at the pubs. Sometimes they get wedged, and their wheels have to be jacked up to part them. One day a milk lorry hit a beer lorry, and our gutters were running with milk one side and pale ale on the other.

This street and its traffic are a symbol of how go-ahead England is in some ways, and how backwards in others. For nobody has yet got around to making a by-pass round our town. *[They did in 1981]*
Adrian Bell, A Street in Suffolk, *(1964), pp.11–12.*

Westerfield Green

Enclosure in Suffolk, for the most part, had taken place by 1600, leaving only the roadside wastes, commons and greens for the 18th century improvers. Here at either end of the county, the loss of the village green is lamented.

What we, perhaps erroneously, consider the baneful spirit of enclosure has extended itself to this pleasant and sequestered village; for, in our memory, Westerfield Green, consisting of several acres, was the annual scene of rural festivity. Cricket-matches – foot-ball – donkey-races, and other rustic amusements, took place upon this spot, which was a favourite resort of the population of Ipswich and the surrounding villages. We remember with delight, these manly sports and pastimes of Westerfield races, and regret that the labouring classes are so much deprived of the power of enjoying them, for we believe that these occasional relaxations from labour, rendered the poor man contented with his lot, and the Common, or the Village Green, contributed to the maintenance of his family, which now, alas! he is compelled to seek from the parish. The Swan public-house is no more, and the Green is enclosed.
G. R. Clarke, The History and Description of the Town and Borough of Ipswich, *(1830), p. 335.*

'No peasant had pin'd at his lot
Tho' new fences the lone heath enclose;
For, alas! The blest days are forgot,
When the poor had their sheep and their cows.
Still had labour been blest with content,
Still competence happy had been,
Not indigence utter'd a plaint,
Had avarice spar'd but the Green!'
Nathaniel Bloomfield, Honington Green, *(1803).*

The Green: Then and Now

Like many another Suffolk village, that in which I spent some part of my childhood used to be so unassuming that its charms were scarcely ever noticed . . .

In the last few decades a superficial metamorphosis has taken place in which once-considered charms have been prettied up and the bucolic face of the village has become prim and proper to face a different world.

Look at The Green for example. As I remember it, long before it became tamed and titivated by Best-Kept-Village mentality, The Green was a rare piece of wild, common waste. It had a couple of ponds fringed with bramble and blackthorn where coot and water-rat could live in tolerable peace when boys were not fishing. Skylarks used to sing high up over the drifts of dog-daisies and waist-high buttercups; a partridge regularly reared its young from the nest on the edge of a hollow pitted with rabbit burrows.

Now all such vulgarities have gone – the very primness of The Green would repulse wild life even if it had not been destroyed already by poison sprays, myxomatosis and the like. At least, they say, The Green is tidy. Tidy, too, is the churchyard which has been razed and reduced to something of complete insignificance and all of it for the convenience of the motor mower. The hedge banks have been tidied with weed-killer and leaves have been tidied by cutting down trees.

What has been lost? Nothing that can be calculated. All that has gone is the nebulous quality of undisciplined nature – so rich and effulgent once that it flowed and flooded in great waves of insect-humming odour into the houses and lives of country people.

It was this that escaped some time during the tidying-up, an essence that disappeared so quietly that no one can say exactly when it happened and so completely that no one could ever expect to know it again.

H. Mills West, 'Percy's Stand', Suffolk Tales, (1982) pp. 26–27.

Middleton Street : 1944

But our street is the hub of our universe. Here is the church, set on the one bit of ground rise in our marshes, which tells the tale of centuries in its varying windows – no two alike – its thatched roof and the chevron-leaded spire that rises above its old flinted battlemented tower that holds a peal of five bells and many bats . . .

The interior of our church is simple. You will look in vain for tombs of the mighty – recumbent knights in armour and great ladies in alabaster – they are not here; you must look farther afield for these, although at no great distance for all that. Our parish is one of humble folk only, with never a one rising above the middle class. However, it has a singer's gallery and a wheezy organ of the barrel variety that has ground out Te Deums and Magnificats and accompanied 'voices ben small, subtill, thicke, clere, sharpe and shrill' through and over those neat little inch-square balusters, and the Royal Arms that give it dignity. Then, of course, being insular, we have a special Suffolk font, with woodhouses and lions complete; not forgetting its faded black inscription, 'Cryst mote us spede, And helpe alle at need.'

The bit of ragged coco matting that runs up the one and only aisle, covers up the white flat bricks, and the ancient graves, including a couple of brasses, small and dark, of which it said that the 'female face is best preserved'; which is perhaps by way of a parable. And then on goes the matting to the Holy Table – made in Stuart times; past the poppy-heads of the pews, and the village carpentry of the reading desk and the pulpit. No rood screen, not a vestige, save the doorway to the loft; but there is an unusual piscine and a sedilia, while at the South door is a Mass clock. But I have not told you of St. Christopher who looks down from the wall with his very fresh face in spite of his years; of the little Christ that still rests on his shoulders; of his staff, and of the boat that fades away into the whitewash, out of which the master's magic was retrieved at some grand clean up. A few memento mori, niches, mullions and mouldings, and the tale is told.

And gathered about the old walls, shut in by another old wall of flint and rubble, capped by neat arched bricks, lie the rude forefathers of the hamlet, under those hummocks and lichened memorials or leaning grave boards. And there's nice little bit of haysel each year, for he who cares to scythe and gather, for it's rich soil in this 'stent'! 'And is it not true that a ground sweat cures all disorders'?

Next the church comes the chapel; and in many respects is of more importance, for we are a strong nonconformist body here. A square-faced building of red brick, flanked by two doors, fronted by a few iron railings, it resembles much the design you would expect to find on a box of bricks. Squared small panes of glass make up its windows in the front, thus adding to the squareness and underlining the principles here taught. But at the rear, in the wall which frames the preacher, and towards which the congregation fastens its eyes, is an example, in duplicate, of country Gothic, in two windows with lancet heads. A panelled gallery, supported on neat little iron pillars, runs round three sides. Another example of country ambition in architecture is found in the battlemented vestry which has been built on to the side presented to the flanking road...

But 'my heart,' they can 'whooly' sing in this Bethel. One never need be in doubt as to whether a 'sarvice' is in progress. You can hear it on the headlands, and down in the 'mashes'; there's no mistaking it; led at one time by a flute, bass violin and clarionet, later by a wheezy harmonium. Wesley made his people sing, and we follow Wesley hereabouts...

And if there was any rivalry among the preachers; if, for instance you should say that 'owd John preached better than Button'; well, then you would be told that Button could 'pray John's head off.'

Here, too, the children came to Sunday school to be taught by old, old people with shining faces and warm hearts. To supplement a meagre acquaintance with the three R's, and to sit 'right still', or to have their ears boxed, or to be reached after by 'a whooly long owd stick.'

Discreetly tucked away in the corner, so that the casual visitor can hardly see it, is the Bell, with its thatched roof, timbered ceilings and capacious cellar. Here the ringers come to whet their whistle, and here, too, the preachers at the chapel baited their hosses, while they held forth between the hymns.

On that little bit of a slope that ends with the churchyard gate is our one and only shop; founded, built up and maintained by Joseph Broom. Here, from a packman's bundle, has grown a marvellous store of all things which a countryman can need, and here is a social centre that rivals even the pub. You can often pick up a bit of news here that might have escaped your acute country ears, for you never knew who you might meet when you unsnecked the door and twanged the bell. Saturday night found a rare clack a going on, that bull's eyes and bacca failed to stem. And sure enough you could find a cap for the boy Jonah, and a pair of mittens for the girl Susie; to say nothing of one of the grey powders for grandfather. And as Joe would say,--'You will catch more flies with a spoonful of honey, than with a gallon of vinegar!'

The old rectory which stands beside where the old tithe barn stood is now let off as a two-dweller, a new rectory, time of the Georges, having been built amid the trees lower down the road. A nice little bit of squareness, this latter, with its gardens all carefully laid out by an early and wealthy rector, with a magnolia-grandiflora before its neatly pillared porticoed doorway. Copper beeches and firs, and the glass lean-to that runs along the south side full of flowers, make up a satisfying whole. The kitchen garden, not forgetting the strawberry bed, is at the rear, separated from our meandering river by the stables and the trees.

Allan Jobson, Suffolk Yesterdays, *(1944), pp. 23–27.*

Yanks at Debach and Grundisburgh : 1942

In the Second World War East Anglia was the site of scores of English and American airbases. The Americans arrived to set up the bases in 1942. One of the airmen, Robert Arbib, gives his first impressions of Suffolk and its people.

Our official welcome to England did not come until our third night at Debach (we pronounced it Deb'-itch) in eastern Suffolk – when we decided to wander, against strict regulations, into the countryside, and see just what this England was like.

It was a joy just to walk through the soft Suffolk countryside those late August evenings. The site for our aerodrome was on top of a plateau of high ground – a rounded hilltop perhaps two miles across. In all directions the roads wound down from it, curving between high hawthorn hedgerows lined with ancient trees, between fields that were ripe with grain, fields that were a sea of clover, or the bright sulphur of mustard. Most fields were cultivated and ready for harvest, but a few were left for cattle to graze and these were the brightest of emerald green. The cattle were sleek and well tended; the horses, those red-brown, blond-maned Suffolk punches, were sturdy and capable.

Here and there farm cottages were hidden behind the hedges and masses of rose vines, with thatch roofs and plaster of that pastel pink or yellow which is so typical of the East Anglian scene. And over all, a pastoral sweetness in the air – mingled with the remote, half-imagined tang of the sea.

It was an age-ripened countryside of almost park-like neatness, and it seemed remote from the war, those first few days. As we walked down the lane towards the village of Grundisburgh, people nodded at us from their gates and waved from their bicycles, and everyone said 'Good evening.' We remarked how very incongruous we must have looked – American soldiers in the midst of this most British, most bucolic magnificence.

The road curled down the hill around a rambling farm, made several lazy turns in a hollow, climbed up against the side of the ridge between rows of cottages, and brought us to a crossroads, marked by a bright-red telephone booth. This crossroads and its half-dozen houses was Burgh. At the crossroad we took the right fork, and the land dipped swiftly downhill between high hedges, made a very sharp and narrow turn right at the bottom, where an indiscreet truck would (and later did) take the corner off a pretty cottage. A left turn then, across the bridge over the brook, a right turn, a left past Grundisburgh Hall, where local legend said that Keats wrote some of his poetry, and you were in the village of Grundisburgh.

Grundisburgh (if you lived there long enough you called it Grunsbra) was a compact village of brick cottage, with a church, a general store-post office, and a public house called 'The Dog' all surrounding a triangular green, through which flowed the brook.

When we entered the little pub, it was almost empty. We found three or four small, plain rooms with wooden benches and bare wooden tables. Each room connected somehow with a central bar – either across a counter or through a tiny window. One of the rooms had a dart board, and another had an antique upright piano. We went into the room with the dart board and ordered beer . . .

Someone must have seen us go into 'The Dog', for soon the villagers began to arrive. By ones and twos they came, and sat themselves down in their accustomed seats. The front room with the dart board filled with the younger men – the farm workers in their rough clothes, talking their musical dialect that puzzled us. In Norfolk they call it 'Norfolk canary.' But in Suffolk it is a twittering close-lipped sing-song too.

The back room filled with the old gaffers, and their evil-smelling pipes filled the room with blue smoke and the smell of burning seaweed. Here the conversation was slower – in fact it bordered on paralysis in social intercourse. A remark was made at one side of the table. Then would follow a long silence. Finally from the other side of the room would come the answer. A chuckle, glasses would be lifted slowly, quaffed, carefully set down, the pipes would be sucked, and then the third comment would come from deep in the corner. There was no need for these old men to hurry. Decades of hard work had brought them a deserved time for relaxation.

Here was contentment, companionship, a time for thinking, and for the slow exchange of ideas. For years they had occupied the same chairs, drank the same pint of bitter from the same silver mugs, talked about the crops, the weather, the latest village gossip, and now another war. Mr. Watson [the landlord]could set his old clock by their entrances. He handed them their brimming mugs of 'the usual' with the expected and customary greeting, took their coppers with a nod. These were his 'regulars.'

But this Saturday evening there was excitement and a high tempo in every room in 'The Dog'. The Yanks have arrived! There are seven of them in 'The Dog' right now! People came in from all the farms and cottages and they filled the old public house with a carnival spirit. By eight o'clock there was standing room only, and by nine o'clock even the dark narrow hall between the rooms was full, and you could hardly turn around. The smoke was thick, and the conversation excited.

The Yanks have arrived! The work on our aerodrome is about to begin at last! It has begun already! Right here, in changeless old Gaunsbra we are going to have a great new bomber aerodrome, and thousands of American soldiers and airmen! And bombers flying right over Berlin to pay those Jerries back! Surely the tide of war is changing today!

Robert Arbib, Here We Are Together, *(1946), pp.58-61.*

5 · THE COAST

Suffolk Holiday Resorts : 1903

The scenery in and around the Suffolk seaside resorts is neither grand nor romantic, but in its quiet charm there is an attraction that grows upon acquaintance; and the effect of the invigorating East Anglian air as a tonic to jaded town-dwellers is becoming so widely appreciated, that were the scenery of these little towns less interesting than it is, the bracing qualities of their climate would still bring them to the front as health resorts.

But the towns along the Suffolk coast have other attractions than their air. The leafy shades of flower-decked Felixstowe, with its good sands, and the beauties of the neighbouring Orwell; the sunniness of air-swept Southwold and Dunwich, with their expanses of purple heather lands and their historical ruins; the quaintness of old-fashioned Aldeburgh, peaceful and secluded, and differing from all other towns in its surroundings of solitary fen and mere, and broad-flowing tidal river with its gorgeous sunset effects – all have their charms. The better they are known the greater becomes their fascination.

Ward Lock, A Pictorial and Descriptive Guide to Aldeburgh, Southwold and Felixstowe, *(1903), pp. ix-x.*

Respectable Lowestoft

Clement Scott did much to promote 'Poppy Land', the coastal area of Norfolk. At Lowestoft, the 'pink of propriety', he is amazed to find an innovation – free shelters for visitors.

I shall always look upon Lowestoft as the very pink of propriety. It is certainly the cleanest, neatest, and most orderly seaside spot at which I have ever cast anchor. There is an air of respectability at the very railway station, no confusion, no touting, no harassing, and no fuss. I am not bothered by hotel porters or omnibus men, or lodging-house keepers or advertisers. When I come to Lowestoft I am expected to know where I am going to, and not to require any further information. I have hardly got into the streets before I discover signs of the same scrupulous order. The shops are prettily arranged, the people are so well disciplined that they always keep in a file to the right or to the left, never running up against or jostling one another on the pathway or foot-bridge, and so considerate are the Lowestoft Improvement Commissioners that they actually provide visitors with a wooden summer-house or shelter in case they should be tired or caught in a shower before they arrive on the beach. Literally this is no exaggeration. At convenient corners of the town are erected shelters or rooms provided with tables and benches, where, without paying a farthing, anyone can rest or converse without impeding the traffic . .

Let me once more call attention to the trim and bandbox appearance of breezy Lowestoft. Not Folkestone, with its Lees, or Sandgate, with its villas, can compete with the Dutch cleanliness, the symmetry, and the precision of this treeless, sunny promenade. Lowestoft, of course, has its pier, not one of those meaningless, lengthy jetties that jut out into the sea and so seriously disfigure the prospect, not a stretch of boards and piles, with a beginning, a middle, and an ending that can be indefinitely prolonged, but a pier that is attached to a harbour, a pier that encloses a basin, a pier with a miniature lighthouse at the end of it, a pier at whose side yachts lie at anchor and from whose steps gaily dressed young ladies start to row or sail these sunny afternoons. Let me be very particular on this point. No one would dream of going out for a sail until after luncheon. The morning is for the sand, the afternoon for the pier, the sunset for the promenade, and the evening once more for the band and the pier.

The afternoon pier is the occasion for the great Lowestoft baby show. The band plays, and the infants are trotted out for inspection. You can see that they have all been carefully groomed; the nurse and nursery governess have been diligently at work to remove the traces of the early dinner. Up and down the children walk, with their dolls and toys, between an avenue of delighted and envious parents...

Let it be remembered that these are all middle-class people of the highest respectability; no tripper or excursionists mingle in these domestic rites; the baby who screams is smothered in lace and insertion; the young gentleman who has a difference with his nurse is in a white sailor suit of unexceptional spotlessness. When they have duly exhibited their children – and their respective tempers – listened to the band, gone out for a shilling or sixpenny sail, and duly gossiped on a pier, without shelter and exposed to the fiercest afternoon sun, they all go indoors at a moment when life is beginning to be endurable in the open air.

This course is, however, necessary in order to prepare for the most delightful feature of a Lowestoft day – the evening pier, when the babies are in bed, and Lowestoft, select and respectable as it is, can indulge in those harmless reveries, flirtations, and repartees that make seaside life endurable. The band plays merrily from its kiosque in the middle, and strange to say, not at the end of the pier; a breeze springs up from the sea and makes one forget the almost intolerable heat: the yachts and pleasure boats rock in the little harbour; the waves plash up against innumerable keels; backwards and forwards go the procession in the semi-darkness; some become sentimental, and many more meditative, until, with perfect punctuality, the concert is brought to a close, and, as if by clockwork, all Lowestoft is moved off to an early bed.

Clement Scott, Poppy-Land, *(1886), pp. 104–11*

Herrings at Lowestoft : 1909

Lowestoft's oldest industry, its sea fishery, is still that for which it is most famous, and during every week of the year the scenes presented by its spacious docks, wharves, and fishmarkets abound in interest. A hundred years ago there were only about forty Lowestoft boats, each carrying a crew of ten or twelve men, regularly engaged in the herring fishery, and a local trawl fishery can hardly be said to have existed; now the Lowestoft fleet of steam and sailing drifters, or boats engaged in herring catching, is one of the finest in the world, and the local fleet of trawlers, consisting of both steamers and smacks, is an equally fine one. In 1907 no fewer than 539 drift-net fishing-boats and trawlers were registered at this port, and during the autumn herring fishing, which commences in September and is continued until a few days before Christmas, from four hundred to five hundred Scotch fishing-boats also have their headquarters here. In that season hundreds of fishing-boats spread their nets almost every night on the fishing grounds, and when they arrive in port the market is often covered with gleaming heaps of silvery herrings, all of which, in the course of a few hours, are bought by the merchants and curers, a considerable portion of them being exported to the Continent, chiefly to Germany, Russia, Belgium and Italy.

In the packing and kippering of the herrings several hundred Scotch 'kipper' girls are employed, and the presence of these 'bonnie lassies,' who are brought by special trains from the North, is an attractive feature of the town during the latter part of the year. Almost as soon as the herrings are landed, they are conveyed to the yards or sheds of the curers, where the girls by the dexterous use of small knives with short, curved blades, prepare them for the process of kippering. Other herrings, not subjected to this splitting process, are suspended in curing sheds, and, after being smoked by the kindling of wood fires beneath them, are ready for sale as the familiar 'bloaters'; while yet others, smoked and dried for longer periods, become the highly flavoured 'reds' or high-dried herrings . . .

Midsummer herrings, which contain little or no roe, are also highly esteemed for their delicate flavour. It is an old saying, the truth of which no East Coast herring fisher will deny, that 'of all fish in the sea the herring is king' . . .

W. A. Dutt, The Norfolk and Suffolk Coast, (1909), pp.11–13.

Southwold and Walberswick: 1899

In the 1880s Wilson Steer produced a series of Impressionist paintings of Walberswick beach, mud flats and village. It then became a fashionable artists' colony and retreat for the middle classes.

Southwold – A delightfully breezy place is this charming Suffolk seaside resort, almost free as yet from all modern devices and abominations. It has a picturesque old-world look about it. Pretty villas, with balconies, standing in trim lawns, are all around us, and a raised terrace overlooking the beach and sea, which must be a great delight to promenaders. The beach below is full of fishing smacks and trim yachts and pleasure boats, and red-tiled huts, which serve as boat-houses, or are associated with some of the mysteries of fishing. And here, positively, is a battery on the raised terrace, no earthwork construction, but long, black-looking naked guns, with their muzzles pointing seawards...

We are now in Walberswick, a little disappointed with the cottages as we enter the place; but presently comes the picturesque little bit of village green, and in another minute we are on the crisp turf which fringes the shore. This is the Walberswick of our dreams – this is the delightful old-world place which we have seen depicted on the walls of so many of our art galleries. Here are the veritable rich bits of colouring, the darkly-stained boards of the wooden houses and the red-tiled roofs, the picturesquely painted barges and fishing boats, the little old-fashioned wooden pier, with the sea dashing against it, the river Blyth, with its ferry and broad current, and white-winged yachts in the distance; but its waters are now at half ebb, and running swiftly down to the sea, to mingle with the grey-green of the German Ocean. Yes, this is really Walberswick . . .

The waters of the Blyth are fresh and green, and sparkling in the sunshine; the red tiles on the black-boarded cottages and outbuildings are rich and vivid in colour; dazzling and white are the sails of the yacht sailing up the reach towards Blythburgh, and the white foam is flashing at the mouth of the river. A glorious morning indeed, and already there are some lady artists at work by the water-courses, and others coming over in the ferry boat with their easels and paint boxes . . .

William Tate, East Coast Scenery, *(1899), pp. 70, 73, 112.*

Dunwich

Human bones from long abandoned churchyards can still be seen in, and at the base of Dunwich cliffs. The 'hollow tower', of the second verse, is all that was left of All Saints church, perched on the cliff edge.

Church and hospice wrought in faultless fashion,
    Hall and chancel bounteous and sublime,
Wide and sweet and glorious as compassion,
    Filled and thrilled with force of choral chime,
Filled with spirit of prayer and filled with passion,
    Hailed a God more merciful that Time . . .

Here is all the end of all his glory –
    Dust, and grass, and barren silent stones.
Dead, like him, one hollow tower and hoary
    Naked in the sea-wind stands and moans,
Filled and thrilled with its perpetual story;
    Here, where earth is dense with dead men's bones . . .

Now displaced, devoured and desecrated,
    Now by Time's hands darkly disinterred,
These poor dead that sleeping here awaited
    Long the archangel's re-creating word,
Closed about with roofs and walls high-gated
    Till the blast of judgement should be heard . . .

Tombs, with bare piteous bone protruded,
    Shroudless, down the loose collapsing banks,
Crumble, from their constant place detruded,
    That the sea devours and gives not thanks.
Graves where hope and prayer and sorrow brooded
    Gape and slide and perish, ranks on ranks.

Rows on rows and line by line they crumble,
    They that thought for all time through to be.
Scarce a stone whereon a child might stumble
    Breaks the grim field paced alone of me.
Earth, and man, and all their Gods wax humble
    Here, where Time brings pasture to the sea.

Algernon Swinburne, Selections from Poetical Works, *(1887), pp. 28-29.*

At Thorpe, near Aldeburgh : 1899

The village of Thorpe was transformed between 1910 and 1928 into a 'Garden Village and model holiday hamlet by the sea.' This description evokes the village before its transformation into a brick and timber Tudor fantasy with houses, almshouses, church and colonial style 'club'.

I have come to Thorpe, a quaint little hamlet on the Suffolk coast. If ever a place gave an impression of being dropped from the clouds, that place is Thorpe.

The houses have been built haphazard, facing north, south, east, or west, at the sweet will of their owners or architects. There is no street, there is only one shop; the Whiteley of Thorpe, its owner, is indeed the universal provided of the place. He is post-master and ginger-beer retailer. He sells marmalade and bathing drawers, liquorice sticks and indiarubber shoes. He owns the one bathing machine of Thorpe, and possesses a chaise and a pony, which, for absolute slowness of progression, would even beat a South-Eastern train, and that is saying much. There is a coastguard station, where two or three devoted servants of her Majesty take turns at looking through a telescope at a passing steamer or the bathers on the shore, the latter for choice, being the rarer sight. There is a tiny convalescent home, which has at present one inmate. How anyone could be ill in such a healthy place I haven't found out. I fancy the poor soul must be an importation. I suppose the natives may occasionally fall sick; perhaps they sometimes even die; but as there is no graveyard or doctor, there is consequently no evidence to the effect that they ever do. And if, of course, Faust-like, they keep their youth for ever, that would account for their being no 'spirits' in Thorpe. No use here for enterprising distillers to advertise their choicest blends of Scotch or Irish, since such cannot be retailed! The one little inn – 'The Crown' – is only licensed for beers, and at the early hour of ten each evening the roisterers of Thorpe have to forsake the sanded floor of their little pub's bar parlour and find their way across the sand-hills to their cottages.

Yes, existence is ideally primitive at this little fishing village. There is no electric-lit parade: the only promenade is the wave-washed shore; there is not even a street lamp: the only light I have seen at night here is that of a million stars and a crescent moon; there are no bands or strolling singers, but there is the never-ceasing music of the sea, and the song of the lark by day only gives way to the plaintive cry of the lapwing or the seagull at dusk; there is neither church nor telegraph office, but there is a sermon preached to you at every step you take on the heath-covered moorland; there is a message telegraphed to you in every crash of those billows on the beach.

The men of Thorpe are nearly all engaged in lobster fishing, and their life is by no means a bed of roses, but they never hesitate when the signal comes to hurry over the two miles of sand-hills that divide Thorpe from Sizewell to join their comrades there and launch their lifeboat into the wildest sea to rescue either passengers or sailors from the many wrecks that happen so frequently on this wild and exposed coast. Both the Sizewell and Aldeburgh lifeboats bear splendid records for life-saving. Aldeburgh is only two miles from Thorpe by the shore, though nearly five by the high-road. A picturesque mere lies between the two places, and it is difficult to recognise that this shallow lagoon, studded with a hundred islands and haunted by wild duck, was once a big tidal creek, where the Dutch eel-boats lay. The face of this coast is being vastly altered by the sea, and a shallow, sandy stream is all that is left of the once big tidal channel that connected the mere with the sea . . .

T. West Carnie, Quaint East Anglia, (1899), pp. 55–59.

The River and the Quay at Aldeburgh

With ceaseless motion comes and goes the Tide,
Flowing, it fills the Channel vast and wide;
Then back to Sea, with strong majestic weep
It rolls, in ebb yet terrible and deep:
Here Sampire-Banks and Salt-wort bound the Flood,
There Stakes and Sea-weeds withering on the mud;
And higher up, a ridge of all things base,
Which some strong tide has roll'd upon the place.

Far other Craft our prouder River shows,
Hoys, Pinks and Sloops; brigs, Brigantines and Snows:

Nor Angler we on our wide stream descry,
But one poor Dredger where his Oysters lie:
He cold and wet and driving with the Tide,
Beats his weak arms against his tarry side,
Then drains the remnant of diluted gin,
To aid the warmth that languishes within,
Renewing oft his poor attempts to beat
His tingling fingers into gathering heat.

He shall again be seen when Evening comes,
And social parties crowd their favourite rooms;
Where, on the Table Pipes and Papers lie,
The steaming Bowl or foaming Tankard by;
'Tis then, with all these comforts spread around,
They hear the painful Dredger's welcome sound;
And few themselves the savoury boon deny,
The food that feeds, the living luxury.

Yon is our Quay! Those smaller Hoys from Town,
Its various Wares, for Country-Use bring down;
Those laden Waggons, in return, impart
The Counry-Produce to the City Mart:
Hark! O the Clamour in that miry Road,
Bounded and narrow'd by yon Vessels' Load;
The lumbering Wealth she empties round the place,
Package and Parcel, Hogshead, Chest and Case:
While the loud Seaman and the angry Hind,
Mingling in Business, bellow to the wind.

Near these a Crew amphibious in the Docks,
Rear, for the Sea, those Castles on the Stocks:
See! The long Keel, which soon the Waves must hide
See! The strong Ribs which form the roomy Side,
Bolts yielding slowly to the sturdiest stroke,
And Planks which curve and crackle in the smoke.
Around the whole rise cloudy Wreathes and far
Bear the warm pungence of o'er boiling Tar.
Revd George Crabbe, The Borough, (1810), pp. 4–6.

To The Deben.

No stately villas, on thy side,
May be reflected in thy tide;
No lawn-like parks, outstretching round,
The willing loiterer's footsteps bound
By woods – that cast their leafy shade,
Or deer that start across the glade;
No ruined abbey, grey with years,
Upon thy marge its pile uprears;
Nor crumbling castle, valour's hold,
Recalls the feudal days of old.

Nor dost thou need that such should be,
To make thee, Deben, dear to me:
That hast thine own befitting charms,
Of quiet heaths, and fertile farms,
With here and there a copse to fling
Its welcome shade, where wild birds sing;
Thy meads, for flocks and herds to graze;
Thy quays and docks, where seamen raise
Their anchor and unfurl their sail
To woo and win the favouring gale.

And, above all, for me thou hast
Endearing memories of the past!
Thy winding banks, with grass o'er-grown,
By me these forty years well known,
Where, eve or morn, 'tis sweet to rove,
Have oft been trod by those I love;
By those who, through life's by-gone hours,
Have strewed its thorny path with flowers,
And by their influence made thy stream
A grateful poet's favourite theme.
Bernard Barton, Household Verses, *(1845), pp. 234–35.*

Felixstowe in 1898

Felixstowe was developed in the 1870s by Col. George Tomline of Orwell Park. But it was the visit of the Empress of Germany in 1891 and, the discovery of spa water a few months later, that gave the real impetus to its popularity as the 'Queen of the East Coast Resorts.'

Picturesque health-giving Felixstowe, with its yellow sands, its verdure-clad cliffs, its wide golfing links, its magnificent climate, its splendid marine views, and its excellent accommodation for visitors, is certainly modern in every sense of the word.

The writer had not visited it for two years, when, on a bright, fine morning toward the end of May, 1898, he went down to see its cheery inhabitants, and to spend a few restful hours within its borders.

What marvellous changes had taken place in this period. Everything seemed new. New Station, new Churches, new Cliff Gardens, new Shelters, new Hotels, new Shops, and new residence of very description. The unpicturesque had become modernised and made beautiful. 'Forward' has been the watchword for the residents of this rising resort, and 'forward' they have moved in consequence. There is no lagging behind here, and it only requires a few more years to make it – as it deserves to be – one of the most popular watering-places on the East Coast – not popular in the sense that one holiday resort was recently described: 'As lively, snobby, a nimble giggling young place,' but popular in the sense of being up-to-date, and yet select and fashionable.

In the summer of 1891, Felixstowe received much attention in all the daily and illustrated papers of Europe on account of the visit to it by the Empress of Germany and her family with her suite in attendance. Her Majesty had been attracted by the fame of this health-giving resort, and the imperial family resided for a month in the picturesque 'Beach' Mansion at the foot of Bent Hill (through the agency of Messrs. W. G. Archer and Son). Fortunately the weather during her visit was delightfully fine, and the five little princes could be seen every day bathing, boating, and sand-digging, untroubled by inquisitive lookers-on. The Imperial Party reached Felixstowe in the German Royal Yacht, Hohenzollen, which afterward lay in Felixstowe docks.

Lemmon Lingwood, Jarrold's Guide to Felixstowe, (1898), pp. 30–34, 39–40.

6 · AGRICULTURAL LABOURERS

The Poetic and Realistic Views of Agricultural Life

Revd George Crabbe depicted everday life, in and around his native town of Aldeburgh, based on the reality of what he saw. He describes not the idyllic life of swain and shepherd, but the harsh and unremitting struggle of agricultural life.

I grant indeed that fields and flocks have charms
For him that grazes or for him that farms;
But when amid such pleasing scenes I trace
The poor laborious natives of the place,
And see the mid-day sun, with fervid ray,
On their bare heads and temples play;
While some, with feebler heads and fainter hearts,
Deplore their fortune, yet sustain their parts—
Then shall I dare these real ills to hide
In tinsel trappings of poetic pride?
  No; cast by Fortune on a frowning coast,
Which neither groves nor happy valleys boast;
Where other cares than those the Muse relates,
And other shepherds dwell with other mates;
By such examples taught, I paint the Cot,
As Truth will paint it, and as bards will not.
Nor you, ye Poor, of letter'd scorn complain,
To you the smoothest song is smooth in vain;

O'ercome by labour, and bow'd down by time,
Feel you the barren flattery of a rhyme?
Can poets soothe you, when you pine for bread,
By winding myrtles round your ruin'd shed?
Can their light tales your weighty griefs o'erpower,
Or glad with airy mirth the toilsome hour?
  Lo! where the heath, with withering brake grown o'er,
Lends the light turf that warms the neighbouring poor;
From thence a length of burning sand appears,
Where the thin harvest waves its wither'd ears;
Rank weeds, that every art and care defy,
Reign o'er the land, and rob the blight'd rye:
There thistles stretch their prickly arms afar,
And to the ragged infant threaten war;
There poppies nodding, mock the hope of toil;
There the blue bugloss paints the sterile soil;
Hardy and high, above the slender sheaf,
The slimy mallow waves her silky leaf;
O'er the young shoot the charlock throws a shade,
And clasping tares cling round the sickly blade;
With mingled tints the rocky coasts abound,
And a sad splendour vainly shines around.
Revd George Crabbe, 'The Village' (1783), in George Crabbe, The Poetical
Works of Rev. George Crabbe, (1840), vol ii, pp. 76–77.

Employment of Boys and Girls in Victorian Suffolk

John Glyde of Ipswich was an early social historian, who collected information and statistics about his own time. Here he combines his own researches with Parliamentary Reports of 1843 to produce this summary of children's working conditions.

A very large number of children are employed at farm labour in this county. Both sexes are sent to the fields early in life to add to the scanty income of the family. John Pearson, Esq., of Framlingham, says: 'Every person in the parish employ children in crow-keeping. I dare say at one time we had 50 or 60 children employed in crow-keeping.' In Hartismere, Hoxne, Woodbridge, Plomesgate, and

Blything Unions, children are very generally employed.

Much depends on the size of the child and the necessities of the family as to the age at which BOYS are first employed, but as proof of the tender age at which work is commenced in this county, we name that at Mildenhall the witness said, 'In some places (in summer) they begin as early as six years of age.' A gentleman at Wickhambrook observes, 'At the age of seven and upwards they go bird-keeping and picking weeds off the land.' Mr. Moore of Badley said, 'Boys sometimes come at 2d. a day; little things that can hardly walk come with their fathers'; and Mr. Lane of Framlingham testified that children sometimes go to work at six years of age, they usually go at seven. In many districts, however, nine and ten years of age are most common to commence work.

The kind of work in which they are engaged varies in different districts. They are generally engaged in weeding, corn-dropping, pulling turnips, crow-keeping, and assist in stone-picking, and, except in cases of scrofulous children, injurious effects on the health or constitution of children are seldom observed. In some parts, however, they are employed in carting, doing man's work instead of boy's, attending horses with heavy tumbrils, and their lives are thus frequently endangered.

The wages of boys when they first go out to work, are generally about 1s. a week, in some districts more. In the Blything Union from 3d. to 9d. a day, according to age and ability; Kesgrave, 4d. to 6d. a day; Bungay and Beccles, 2d. to 5d. a day; Stowmarket, 2d. to 4d. a day; Boys tending birds, 1s. 6d. to 2s. 6d. a week according to age.

The out-door employment for GIRLS is precisely the same in kind with that of the women, and only varies in degree according to the age and strength of the children employed. Girls assist their mothers in stone-picking, etc. at an early age, and in keeping birds. They are in some districts more employed than boys, and the elder girls so employed are sometimes absent from school from six to eight months in the year. It employs their Sundays also. Their earnings vary from 2d. to 6d. a day. Girls of sixteen generally earn 6d. a day. At Livermere in some years, there is employment for two or three weeks in gathering acorns, and at Stowmarket the hop-picking is a good harvest for the girls of that district. As much as £1,500 have been spent by the different growers in that Union for picking hops.

A good insight into the out-door work and living is afforded by the following statement:

Hannah Winkup, servant to Mr. Catt of Whitton: I am 15 years – was born at Sibton, near Yoxford. My father was a blacksmith; my mother had 12 children, and one of them was deaf and dumb; went out to work in the fields when I was 12 – keeping birds, sheep or cows; I frequently done boy's work – keeping sheep or cows is to prevent their getting into corn fields. I had 3d. a day; worked Sunday as well, but my master used to give me a dinner on Sunday. Have gone stone-picking, hay making, weeding, and dropping. Earnt 5d. a day at dropping; like hay making best. Stone-picking is the hardest work I done – so much ligging; the stones have frequently to be brought from top to bottom of the field and it is very cold work. I worked from eight o'clock in the morning to six o'clock in the evening. Got my breakfast before I went; was allowed one hour for dinner, from twelve to one; had no more until I went home at six. I had bread and cheese for breakfast and cold coffee, no sugar – same for dinner, and very often the same for supper. At other times mother would boil a dumpling for us for supper, this was in stone-picking time, when we always come home very cold. We were so poor that sometimes I have had to go to bed without a supper; generally had a piece of meat on Sundays not butcher's meat, but pork. Have been in service three quarters of a year; my mistress is very kind to me; she lived in the same village I did; I have £2 10s a year wages, and Missus gave me clothes worth another pound.

There are various other employments for girls in different districts of the county. At Hadleigh about 350 girls are employed in the silk trade. Those under 11 years work 6fi hours daily, those above 11 years old work 10 hours daily, and their wages range from 1s. 9d. to 6s. a week. At Sudbury there are no silk 'mills,' but the winding and weaving branches of the trade are carried on, and girls earn from 3s. to 6s. a week according to capability. Unless, however, they are instructed by their parents at home, they have to be 'apprenticed,' and during that period their earnings are very small. More than 1,000 Suffolk girls are employed as straw plaiters, chiefly in the Risbridge and Sudbury Unions, and most of the mothers of illegitimate children in those districts are straw plaiters. At Eye there are a few girls engaged in lace weaving, but their earnings are a mere trifle. At Glemsford and Melford the weaving of horse-hair for chair bottoms, and also that of cocoa-fibre matting, is carried on. At. Ipswich, stay-making affords employment for a large number of females. In the Blything Union, and along the coast generally, many girls and women earn from 6d. to 1s. a-day by braiding fishing nets in the autumn season. At Sudbury, and neighbourhood, the children assist their parents in weaving; and in Stoke-by-Nayland district, a number of boys and girls are employed in tailoring.

It may be safely affirmed that whatever the work of the locality might be, young children are forced to take their share in it, and to give up the real seed time of their education for a premature and unreasonable harvest, and it will, we fear, be long ere the public are fully sensible of the importance of snatching poverty, even in infancy, from the grasp of that ignorance which destroys its mental sight, to deliver it over the more easily to the fatal guidance of vice.

John Glyde, Suffolk in the Nineteeth Century, (1856), p. 368-72.

Petty Sessions for Hiring of Servants

A century ago, it was customary once a year to hold what was called a 'Petty Sessions' in each of the Hundreds of Suffolk, for the Hiring and Retaining of Servants. The male and female servants used to assemble every Michaelmas at a time and place fixed by the chief constable of the hundred, and the 'Sessions' was generally held at some noted public-house in the district. Thus, for Plomesgate, it was held at the 'Green Man,' Tunstall; for Cosford, at the 'Crown,' Bildeston; for Blackbourn, at the 'Boar,' Walsham le Willlows; for Blything, at Halesworth, sometimes at the 'Tuns,' and sometimes at the 'Angel;' for Bosmere, at the 'Crown,' Coddenham, etc

Old Acts of Parliament had originated this custom by enacting that ploughmen and other labourers should be hired to serve for a full year, and not by the day. The servants open to engagements stood in a row at a particular spot, some of them exhibiting a straw in their mouths, to indicate their unengaged condition. A small sum of money given to each servant was supposed to legalize the contract. When the business of the day was over, amusement began. Dinner was provided at each of the public houses at which the Petty Sessions was held, the best room being laid out with tables and forms for the entertainment of the multitude. The announcement of the dinner always formed part of the advertisement, the stereotype phraseology being, 'Where all persons will meet with a hearty welcome from their humble servant.'

John Glyde, New Suffolk Garland, (1866), pp. 284-85.

Income and Expenditure of a Suffolk Family : 1842

This is a rare survival – the income and expenditure of an agricultural labourer and his family, for a week in 1842. This is the equivalent of our till receipts which we throw away without a thought of their future historical use. Alhough this week may not be typical, it is clear that Robert's wages all went on bread. Mr. Micawber would have been pleased with the balance!

Lavenham: Their diet depends in a great measure upon the number of the family, and the amount of wages brought home to the common stock; whether they are frugal in their habits, and in the outlay of their money, &c. I can give you some information, however, on the subject, having made myself acquainted on different occasions with the manner their wages are disposed of.

The following is an account from a woman whose family always appear clean and neat, and whose children are brought up to industrial habits.

NAME	AGE	EARNINGS		EXPENDITURE		
		s	d		s	d
Robert Crick	42	9	0	Bread	9	0
				Potatoes	1	0
Wife	40	0	9	Rent	1	2
				Tea		2
Boy	12	2	0	Sugar		3½
				Soap		3
Boy	11	1	0	Blue		½
				Thread &c		2
Boy	8	1	0	Candles		3
				Salt		½
Girl	6			Coal and wood		9
				Butter		4½
Boy	4			Cheese		3
TOTAL EARNINGS		13	9	TOTAL EXPENDITURE	13	9

But there are numbers of families who, although in the possession of the amount of wages shown above, do not dispose of it with such frugality, but appear in the greatest state of destitution; many others, with the same number of children, do not get the wages this man's family have. The family I have given as an example is more to show you, that with industry and frugality their diet consists principally of bread and potatoes. There are, however, some who, when their families are grown up, by putting their earnings together, occasionally get a piece of meat at their supper-time, and their Sunday dinner.

Stephen Denison, Enquiry into the Employment of Women and Children in Suffolk, Norfolk and Lincoln, *Parliamentary Papers, (1843) pp. 232–33.*

Cottages on the Helmingham Estate : 1879

The rent of the labourer's cottages at Helmingham is £3.10s a year, each including the flower garden, and a farm rent is charged for the half-acre garden, that is, the same as the adjoining farm paid for the half acre before its enclosure as a garden. I should estimate the cost of each pair of cottages as not very much less than £300. There are pigstyes to each. I am told that the present proprietor [Lord Tollemache] has rebuilt and repaired about 100 cottages on the 7000 and odd acres which comprise his estate here, and he has erected about 100 new cottages. So far as I could learn by observation and enquiry the number of the good cottages is about 200, and the number of the bad is none. The supply of labourers residing in the cottages amounts to about four men per hundred acres. One might be sure, in only ge estate, and glancing at the cottages, that the changes of a new agricultural regime had been effected here. The supply of labour on the spot must have been doubled. What the moral change has been I cannot tell from actual observation, but one may draw comparisons from personal experience elsewhere. All who understand the effect on a rural population of improving the cottages, doubling the number, and adding good gardens, will understand that the change must have been a happy one. Double cottages seem to me to be advantageous. They offer companionship and the opportunity of mutual aid in isolated situations and they are warmer than single cottages, partly in consequence of the central chimney.

Bury and Norwich Post, *21 October, 1879.*

A Back'us Boy in the 1890s

Robert Lionel Savage, the last of a long line of shepherds, is in his seventy-sixth year . . .

He left school at the age of twelve after satisfying the local schools inspector that he had reached a sufficient standard of learning to seek a job. He then went as a back'us (back-house or kitchen boy) to a big farm in the village. The back'us boy was at that time the lowest rank in the rural hierarchy. He was under the command of the farmer's wife. She called and the back'us boy answered; and the calls he answered were many and various. A list of Robert Savage's duties gives an idea of the back'us boy's working day.

He rose at six-thirty in the morning and his first job was to give the milking pails to the cowman. These were kept indoors for the sake of cleanliness and the cowman would have to come to the kitchen door to fetch them. He next made the copper-fire so that there would be plenty of water for the maids to carry upstairs for the family to wash. After the copper came the black-stocks – the open, barred fire-grates which would be lighted either for warmth or for cooking. Then as he turned from the blackstocks he would see numerous pairs of boots and shoes which the maids had set out in the back-kitchen waiting to be cleaned. These were the footwear of the farmer's family and of the guests who happened to be staying in the house; and had to be taken upstairs by the maids before 'they' rose. His next job was to grind coffee for the cook; and he was also under her eye as he did his next job which was cleaning all the knives. The knives were made of steel and they were cleaned daily with bath-brick and a board specially kept for the purpose. He would just have time to feed the fowls before breakfast time at nine o'clock.

The fare for breakfast was usually herrings and salt pork. 'They were wunnerful people for herrings.' The herrings were smoked or bloated and enough were bought to last a week: they were strung up on a line across the back-kitchen. Robert Savage was not happy with the breakfast when he first went to the farm because, as he said 'warm herrings and cold fat pork didn't fare to go right together.'

After breakfast came prayers. The girls filed into the drawing-room first and knelt down at the front. The back'us boy with the groom and any other male members of the household knelt behind them. Robert Savage confessed to tickling the girls in front of him to make them laugh: he was bored during prayers and would loiter over his breakfast purposely to get out of attending them. But after one of the family had read and a hymn had been sung, the servants would be released to their various tasks. The back'us boy's duties now took him outside: first to get the vegetables for dinner – potatoes, cabbages, roots, sparrow-grass (asparagus), anything that was in season. Then he chopped the kindling wood and filled the old brass-bound coal-scuttles and carried them into the house; next he peeled the potatoes for the cook.

Dinner was eaten about one-thirty, after the family had eaten theirs. The fare in the kitchen was left over from the dining-room. In the afternoon the back'us boy fed the fowls again; fetched the cows from the marshes; collected the eggs and did all kinds of jobs about the kitchen – any job that would turn up. Then came tea; and as soon as tea was cleared away and one or two little odd jobs completed, the last task was to take the letters to the post office, about three-quarters of a mile away. This had to be done before six-thirty. If there were no evening jobs he could stay up in the village; this gave him a chance to visit his home or play with his friends. Whatever he did he had to be back at the farm before nine o'clock But on some evenings he had to go back to dig in the garden; or if there were visitors he had to stand by to help with their horses when they went home. This was a better job than digging in the garden as the visitors invariably gave him a tip.

Wages were £1 a quarter . . .

George Ewart Evans, Ask The Fellows Who Cut The Hay, *(1956) pp. 23–25.*

Man versus Machine

It was Tuffy's immense capacity for work that caused wonder and created legend . . . for he attacked whatever farm task came to hand with a kind of nervous violence that 'whooly stammed' the natives and delighted the farmer who employed him. In time he became head man at the farm and would have been Lord of the harvest but for the innovation of the mechanical reapers.

As it was he had often led a team of 15 men into the harvest field, and quickly left them behind as he cut the first swathe with his scythe, 'as fast,' it was said, 'as a man could walk'. But the new reaping machines were already clacking and taking the corn away from the scythes, and as the clacking grew so the mowing team dwindled to mere clearers of the headlands for the convenience of the machine.

Part of Tuffy's enthusiasm for work lay in the particular care and pride he took in his tools. His cutting tools were of the finest that cunning and experience could make, his scythe light and handy with a slim, smooth-grained stale that was the envy of lesser men. 'Why, tha's on'y a doddy little thing' they would say, comparing it with their own heavier scythes and he would answer shortly: 'Lighter the timber, better the blade,' and prove it with the speed of his work. His accomplished mowing was a lesson to all, for the scythe was no easy tool for the beginner to master, and many a one who could only 'cut some, cover some and dozzle some' (dozzle means to stun or stupefy) learned the secret at his hands.

However, it seemed that the day of the mower and the hand-worker generally was coming to an end. It was something that shocked the farm men and drove Tuffy to despair; the day of his personal dominance in the field was over. The time came when in desperation he sought to prove to the farmer that he could equal the achievement of the clacking machine by his own strength and speed with a scythe and nothing would satisfy him but a proper trial in the cornfield.

It was a contest so unequal that the conclusion must have easily been foreseen by all except Tuffy. The reaping machine pulled by two round-bellied Punchs, was to have a handicap of ten yards and the race limited to one swathe across the field.

On a fine morning in early September, Tuffy advanced ten yards into a bay in the cornfield, his sharpened and polished scythe ready and at the signal, set to furiously to the task. Perhaps no one had ever mowed at that speed before, but it was not quick enough for the mechanical reaper. As the hated sound grew nearer Tuffy worked in a frenzy until the horses drew level and then overtook.

Suddenly in the same movement as he cut through the corn, he threw the scythe sideways at the machine. It was a gesture of despair and anger that renounced all that he had believed in and worked for . . .

H. Mills West, 'Tuffy Dean', Suffolk Tales, (1982), pp. 31–33.

7 · THE POOR

Tudor Christmas Charity

Thomas Tusser farmed at Brantham in the 1550s. His book, quoted here, was the standard agricultural text book until the late 17th century. Farmers are encouraged to remember their labourers and the poor at Christmas.

At Christmas, good husbands, have corn on the ground,
In barn and in soller, worth many a pound;
With plenty of other things – cattle and sheep,
All sent them (no doubt on) good houses to keep.

At Christmas, the hardness of winter doth rage,
A griper of all things, and especially age:
Then lightly poor people, the young with the old,
Be sorest oppresed with hunger and cold,

At Christmas, by labor is little to get,
That wanting, the poorest in danger are set;
What season then better, of all the whole year,
Thy needy, poor neighbour to comfort and cheer?

At this time, and that time, some make a great matter;
Some help not, but hinder the poor with their clatter,
Take custom from feasting, what cometh then last?
Where one hath a dinner, a hundred shall fast . . .

Good husband and huswife, now chiefly be glad,
Things handsome to have as they ought to be had.
They both do provide against Christmas to come,
To welcome good neighbour, good cheer to have some.

Good bread, and good drink, a good fire in the hall,
Brawn, pudding, and souse, and good mustard withal:
Beef, mutton and pork, shred pies of the best,
Pig, veal, goose and capon, and turket well drest;
Cheese, apples, and nuts; joly carols to hear,
As then in the country is counted good cheer.

What cost to good husband is any of this?
Good household provision only it is.
Of other the like, I do leave out a many,
That costeth the husbandman never a penny.

At Christmas be merry, and thankful withal,
And feast thy poor neighbour, the great with the small;
Yea, all the year long, to the poor let us give,
God's blessing to follow us while we do live.
Thomas Tusser, Five Hundred Points of Husbandry, *(1571)*

The Poor : 1603

*Robert Reyce looks upon the poor as God's gift, in order that the
better off may be moved to do good works. He also makes the point
that God hears the prayers of the poor and rich alike.*

It is familiar with the nature of man to weigh benefitts received, with
feathers and light weights, butt incommodities, hee weigheth with
lead and heavy weights, complayning evermore with a long and large
report of them, such is the corrupt and froward judgement of many in
these dayes, who esteeme the multitude of our poore heere to bee a
matter of heavy burden, and a sore discommoditie, thinking that as
noe griefe is greater than their owne, so no incommoditie to bee
greater than that which is where they dwell. Butt if such did remember
that as well as the poore as the rich proceed before the Lord, and that

the rich cannott stand withoutt the poore, or if they did see how fare the nomber of the poore in other shires do exceed ours, they would nott esteeme of our poore as a burden, butt as a looking glasse wherein the rich may see his owne estate, if once the Lord should bereave him of his benefitts which hee doth dayly abuse.

Indeed I must say as it hath pleased the Lord to voutsafe vs some poore, so what with the powerfull effort of the prevayling word, and the due regard of the commanding law, much charitable reliefe is heere vsed, so that few there bee that goe vnrelieved, whither they bee poore by impotence or by casualty. As for the thriftles poore, whither hee bee riotous, idle person, or vagabond, the list of the late godly lawes, will so reform the quality of them, or diminish the number of them, that there will bee much spared to add to the reliefe of the other.

Butt God in all ages, and in all places haue appointed the poore to bee as the trial of the rich, and the humble thoughts which smoake from a poore mans cottage are as sweet a sacrifice vnto the Lord as the costly perfumes of the princes palace.

Lord Francis Hervey, (ed), Robert Reyce, The Breviary of Suffolk, (1603), (1902), pp. 56-57.

Sudbury Workhouse : 1845

The New Poor Law had abolished outdoor relief and, all in need, had to go into the new Union Workhouses. George Fulcher of Sudbury, was part of the middle class anti-Poor Law movement. He regarded himself the successor to Crabbe in highlighting the harshness of the workhouse system.

Where yonder fir-trees hang their cones on high,
The Union Poor-House mets the wond'ring eye;
Smooth gravel walks the spacious entrance grace,
And towers and turrets crown the stately place.
The garden, gently sloping to the west,
In nature's beauty is profusely drest,
Flowers of all hues adorn the rich parterre,
And roll their fragrance on the evening air,
Whilst at the lofty mansion's iron gates,
In idle state th' obsequious Porter waits.

Ah! little deem the careless passers-by,
How many a wounded heart goes there to die;
Ah! little deem they, that those huge walls hide
The bitter tears of shame and honest pride,
That there, expiring Hope's last ling'ring sighs
From earth's poor outcasts unregarded rise.
Business or pleasure's all-engrossing power,
Life's thousand cares that ask each fleeting hour,
Leave little leisure in wealth's anxious race,
For pity's claims to take their rightful place.
There, wasting sickness lingers day by day,
And all unheeded gasps her life away;
While hireling nurses watch its ebbing sighs,
Impatient, close the scarcely sightless eyes,
And stretch the stiff'ning limbs ere the tired spirit flies.
George Fulcher, The Village Paupers, *(1845) p.1–2.*

Newmarket Workhouse : 1846

This is a description of a workhouse from a different perspective – by one who was a pauper. James Reynolds, known as the 'Hedgerow Poet,' wrote these lines to his sister from Newmarket Union Workhouse. Although, intended to be humorous, the pathos strikes home when he states he cannot see anything other than the sky from the workhouse yard.

Since I cannot, dear sister, with you hold communion,
I'll give you a sketch of our life in the union.
But how to begin I don't know, I declare:
Let me see: well, the first is our grand bill of fare.
We've skilly for breakfast; at night bread and cheese,

And we eat it and then go to bed if you please.
Two days in the week we have puddings for dinner,
And two, we have broth, so like water but thinner;
Two, meat and potatoes, of this none to spare;
One day, bread and cheese – and this is our fare.

And now then my clothes I will try to portray;
They're made of coarse cloth and the colour is grey,
My jacket and waistcoat don't fit me at all;
My shirt is too short, or I am too tall;
My shoes are not pairs, though of course I have two,
They are down at the heel, and my stockings are blue . . .
A sort of Scotch bonnet we wear on our heads,
And I sleep in a room where there are just fourteen beds.
Some are sleeping, some are snoring, some talking, some playing,
Some fighting, some swearing, but very few praying.

Here are nine at a time that work on the mill;
We take it in turns so it never stands still:
A half hour each gang, so 'tis not very hard,
And when we are off we can walk in the yard . . .

I sometimes look up to the bit of blue sky
High over my head, with a tear in my eye.
Surrounded by walls that are too tall too climb,
Confined like a felon without any crime;
Not a field not a house not a hedge can I see
Not a plant, not a flower, nor a bush nor a tree . . .
But I'm getting I find, too pathetic by half,
And my object was only to cause you a laugh;
So my love to yourself, your husband and daughter,
I'll drink to your health in a tin of cold water:
Of course, we've no wine nor porter nor beer,
So you see that we all are teetotallers here.
James Withers Reynolds, Poems Upon Various Subjects, *(1854), pp. 140-42.*

8 · LEGENDS AND SUPERSTITIONS

The Green Children of Woolpit

There is a village in East Anglia, four or five miles it is said from the noble monastery of the blessed King and martyr Edmund. Next to this village can be seen certain very ancient ditches which in the English tongue are called Wolfpitts, i.e. Wolf pits; and these give the name to the village nearby. From these pits, at harvest time with the harvesters busy in the fields collecting the crops, two children came out, one male and one female, with their whole bodies green and dressed in clothing of unusual colour and material. While they were wandering, amazed through the fields, they were arrested by the harvesters and taken to the village, where many gathered at the sight of such a novelty. For some days they were kept without them eating food. Even when they were almost fainting from hunger they would not touch any of the food offered to them. By chance it happened that beans were being brought in from the fields, which seizing immediately they looked for the pith inside the stalks and when finding nothing in the stalks they wept bitterly. Then one of the bystanders ripped out the pith from a pod and offered it to them; this they took at once and ate it, they lived on this food for some months until they got used to bread. Then gradually their colour changed as the nature of our food affected them and they became like us. They also learned the use of our language.

It seemed a good idea to the wise that the children should receive the sacrament of Holy Baptism. This was done but the boy who seemed the youngest died soon after, leaving his sister who was now not much different from our own women, and it is said that she later married a man from [Kings] Lynn. When they had learned our language and when they were asked who they were; where they had come from? Their answer was that they were from the land of St. Martin, who was highly venerated there. They could not explain where this land was, or how they had got from that land to where they had been found by the villagers. What they did remember was that when they were looking after their Father's herds in the fields, they heard a great noise, just like we now usually hear the bells of the Monastery of St. Edmunds: and while they were wondering about this noise they suddenly found themselves amongst the harvesters in strange surroundings.

When they were asked if there was any belief in Christ their reply was that there was Christianity and that there were churches. To a question about the sun and its movements, the answer was that the sun did not rise in their country, that the amount of light was only small like we have just before sunrise and just after sunset. They did mention that they could clearly see another country from their own, across a very big river. These things and many others, which would take far too long to relate, were answered by the children to those people who had asked. Anyone can say what they like as they puzzle over these things; I am not ashamed to have told this amazing event; indeed this story is too complicated for our intelligence to understand.
William of Newburgh, Historia Rerum Anglicarum, *(c. 1196 - 98), Translation provided by Rod Jones of Woolpit.*

The Wild Man of Orford

In the time of Henry II, when Bartholomew de Glanville was keeper of Orford Castle, it happened that fishermen fishing in the sea there caught a wild man in their nets; who was taken to the aforesaid castellan as a marvel. He was entirely naked, and like a human being in all his limbs. But he had hair, though it seemed on the surface almost torn away and destroyed. His beard was full and pointed, and his chest extremely hairy and shaggy. The aforesaid knight had him guarded day and night for a long time, so that he could not approach the sea. Whatever was brought up to him he ate greedily. He ate fish raw as well as cooked, but he wrung out the raw fish in his hands, until all the liquid had gone, and then ate them. But he would not utter a word or rather could not, even though he was hung up by his feet and often severely tortured. When he was taken to a church, he showed not the least sign of reverence or belief, either by kneeling or bowing his head, when he saw anything holy. He always hurried to his sleeping place at nightfall and slept there until dawn.

It happened that they took him once to the harbour and let him loose in the sea, having placed a triple line of very strong nets across the harbour. He soon made for the depths of the sea, passing all the nets, and repeatedly came up from the deep water, gazing at those who were watching him from the shore for a long time, often diving down and reappearing after a moment, as though he was mocking those who watched him because he had escaped from their nets. He played like this in the sea for a long while, and everyone had given up hope that he would return, but he came back of his own accord to them, swimming though the waves, and remained with them for another two months. But after this he was less carefully guarded, and he now disliked his way of life; so he secretly slipped down to the sea and never appeared again. Whether this was a mortal man or some kind of fish pretending to be a human being or some evil spirit lurking in the body of a drowned man (such as is described in the life of St Ouen) it is not easy to see, particularly as so many people tell such marvellous tales about this kind of event.

Ralph de Coggeshall, Chronicon Anglicanum, (c. 1187 – 1224) in, Rolls Series, (1875) Vol 66, pp. 117-118

Omens, of Luck and Health

There are some persons who will never kill a pig when the moon is 'wasting,' lest the pork should waste in the pot. On the other hand, the clergyman of a country town says, ' I know a respectable old lady who always has her corns cut at that time, supposing that the amputation is both more easy and effectual.'

Amongst the Romans sneezing, under some circumstances, at least, was reckoned ominous of evil; but amongst Suffolk people to sneeze three times before breakfast is a pledge that you will soon have a present made to you. The sneezing of a cat however is considered to be an evil omen; it is a sign that the family of the owner will all have colds.

It is usual in this county to communicate family secrets to the bees, such for instance as a birth or death. If neglected on such occasions, the bees are apt, it is said, to take offence, and to move to other residences where they will be treated with more confidence. They are said to be so sensitive as to leave houses, the inmates of which indulge habitually in swearing.

It is regarded as a bad omen, if when you leave a house you replace the chair on which you have been sitting against the wall; the probability, if not the certainty in this case is that you will never visit that house again.

That certain days are more lucky and auspicious than others is a very prevalent belief in many nations. Some remains of this notion exist among us, in the rural parishes more especially. Friday is considered an unlucky day. Sunday, on the other hand, is regarded as an auspicious day; and if persons have been ill and have become convalescent, they almost always get up for the first time on Sundays.

All medicine should be taken 'next the heart,' which means, in the dialect of Suffolk, that the best time for taking medicine is to take it in the morning, fasting.

A lady who has married, but who has not by marriage changed her maiden name, is the best of all persons to administer medicine, since no remedy given by her will fail to cure.

Persons will take the Bible to bed with them on New Year's Eve, and as soon as they wake after twelve o'clock, they open it at random in the dark, mark a verse with their thumb, or stick a pin through a verse, turn down a corner of a page, and replace the book under the pillow. That verse is supposed to be a prophet of destiny (good or bad) during the coming year.

If a corpse is supple after death, it is a sign that there will be another death in that family before very long.

To break a looking-glass is exceedingly unlucky, and will bring death to yourself or an intimate friend.

A belief in the existence of 'Pharisees,' or 'Fairies,' prevails; they ride young horses about in the night, so that the grooms on going into the stable in the morning find the horses all of a foam. But a hag stone, with a hole through, tied to the key of the stable door, protects the horses.

Belief in death-tokens is very prevalent; three raps at a bed's head, and the howling of a dog in front of your house during the night, are warnings that the death of some member of the family is at hand.

Taking a sprig of blackthorn, when in blossom, into a house, is considered to presage death to some member of the family.

> ' If you sweep the house with blossomed broom in May,
> You're sure to sweep the head of the house away.'

If you break two things, you will break a third. A lady saw one of her servants take up a coarse earthenware basin, and deliberately throw it down on the brick floor. 'What did you do that for?' asked the mistress. 'Because, ma'am, I'd broke tew things,' answered the servant; 'so I thout the third 'd better be this here,' pointing to the remains of the least valuable piece of pottery in the establishment, which had been sacrificed to glut the vengeance of the offended ceramic deities.

John Glyde, New Suffolk Garland, (1866), pp.178-180

Whom Shall I Marry?

The following spell is said to be used by some country maidens in Suffolk:

> 'A clover of two, if you put in your shoe,
> The next man you meet in field or lane
> Will be your husband, or one of the name.'

To ascertain whether her pretended lovers really love her or not, the maiden takes an apple pip, and naming one of her followers, puts the pip in the fire. If it makes a noise in burning, from the heat, it is a proof of love; but if it is consumed without a crack, she is fully satisfied that there is no real regard towards her in the person named.

The kitchen maid, when she shells green-peas, never omits, when she finds one having nine peas, to lay it on the lintel of the kitchen door; and the first male who enters it is infallibly to be her husband, or at least her sweetheart.

If two persons wish to marry, they must take the church key and place it over the sixth and seventh verses of the eighth chapter of the Song of Solomon.

> 'Set me a seal upon thine heart, as a seal upon thine arm; for love is strong as death;   jealousy is cruel as the grave; the coals thereof are coals of fire, which hath a most vehement flame. Many waters cannot quench love, neither can the floods drown it; if a man would give all the substance of his house for love, it would utterly be condemned.'

Over the words they must hold the church key, balancing it by the end; and if the wards of the key incline towards the verses, which by skilful manipulation they can easily be made to do, it is a sign that the course of true love will run smooth.

But if, after all, doubts of the lady's fitness to be his wife take possession of the gentleman's mind, there is another chapter in the Holy Bible which if consulted, will either confirm or scatter them. That chapter is the last in the Book of Proverbs. It contains thirty-one verses, corresponding with the days in the longest months. The hesitating lover must ascertain on what day of the month the lady's birthday falls, and then compare with the verse which agrees with it in number. He will thus find out the kind of life which he will lead with her in the event of marriage; and if the verdict prove unfavourable, he will have an opportunity of avoiding a match which he has such strong reason to believe will not be a happy one...

There is an extraordinary notion in regard to the birth of children. As soon as they are born they ought, it is said, to be carried UP stairs, or they will never rise to riches and distinction in their after life; and accordingly, if there are no attics for the nurse to climb up into, she will sometimes mount upon a chair or stool with the new-born baby in her arms.

John Glyde, New Suffolk Garland, *(1866), pp. 175-177.*

Matthew Hopkins in Suffolk : 1645

Matthew Hopkins was the self-appointed Witch Finder, of the Eastern Association, in 1645. His Puritan faith, a fear of women and a belief in the supernatural may have combined to convince him of his task. Although surviving records are scanty, he seems to have been active throughout Suffolk, with his assistants John Stearn and Goody Phillips. A preliminary hearing was held before a magistrate, who decided if the charge was true or not. If true the prisoner went for trial at the Quarter Sessions or Assizes and if found guilty was hanged.

Alice Warner of Rushmere Frely beeinge at her liberty confessed that she had entertained evill sperits which had succ[l]ed her, and and that she imployed them to carry lice to one Wrights wife and to one Barnies, and the said weamen weare lousie according as she confessed. – True. –

John Lowis [Brandestone] incantations, witness Charles Kno. That after his swimminge at Framingham he confessed in his presence, he havinge showen his markes to this deponent, that the biggest of his imps Thomas for he had 7 Flo bess and Mary did suck at this teate, but beeinge asked if he had made any contract said not, but Tom had sometimes moved in a hollow voyce to that purpose, he beeinge asked how longe these imps had sucked, said 5 years and he said to Tom, who came first to him asked if he shold suck he said when goody [ ] & mother Sherewood weare weary of him he shold suck of him. & further he said the water was inchanted by an other witch, witness daniel Rayner that Lowis confessed he imployed his yellow imp to doe all the hurt he cold at Sea between Yarmouth and Winterton, and that he had been the death of many cattell and that these imps did force him to imploy them about some evill action. Nathaniel Man. of Branson witnesses he that upon fallinge out with Mr. Lowis & Mr. Lowis thretinge him, he went for a warrant to bind him to the pease and that imedeately after, Mr. Lowis came to this deponents wife who haveinge a child with her, he wold give her 2s. 6d. to buy it somethinge and immediately after this money recieued the child fell sick languisehed and though it eate the meate yet it gathered no strength, but so continued until it died: *[Revd John Lowes was hanged at Bury St. Edmunds in August 1645]*

Mary wife of Scrutton of Framlingham, witness Ed. Weetinge, the first night she was taken she had 3 imps that succed her severall times this 3 or 4 month some times 2 or 3 in a day, and that they kept a squeakinge and that one night she heard them on the plan | | and she told her husband there weare mise & answered you company with witches & your plagued. With some of theyr emps, that the devill appeared to her twise once like a beare, once like a cat, and that he tempted her in a hollow voyce to kill her child, and as she was comeinge home lately the devill met her like a man and took her by the arme but wold not confes what he said to her. – True. –
C. L. Ewen, Witch Hunting and Witch Trials, (1929), pp. 291, 300-1, 304.

The Fakenham Ghost

The Lawns were dry in Euston Park;
(Here Truth inspires my tale)
The lonely footpath, still and dark,
Led over Hill and Dale.

Benighted was an ancient Dame,
And fearful haste she made
To gain the vale of Fakenham,
And hail its Willow shade.

Her footsteps knew no idle stops,
But follow'd faster still;
And echo'd to the darksome Copse
That whisper'd on the Hill:

Where clam'rous Rooks, yet scarcely hush'd
Bespoke a peopled shade;
Any many a wing the foliage brush'd
And hov'ring circuits made.

The dappled herd of grazing Deer
That sought the shades by day,
Now started from her path with fear,
And gave the Stranger way.

Darker it grew, and darker fears
Came o'er her troubled mind;
When now, a short quick step she hears
Come patting close behind.

She turns, it stopt ! ... nought could she see
Upon the gloomy plain !
But, as she strove the Sprite to flee,
She heard the same again.

Now terror seiz'd her quaking frame:
For, where the path was bare,
The trotting Ghost kept on the same !
She mutter'd many a prayer.

Yet once again, amidst her fright
She tried what sight could do;
When through the cheating glooms of night,
A MONSTER stood in view.

Regardless of whate'er she felt,
It followed down the plain !
She own'd her sins, and down she knelt,
And said her pray'rs again.

Then on she sped: and Hope grew strong,
The white park gate in view;
Which pushing hard, so long it swung
That Ghost and all pass'd through.

Loud fell the gate against the post !
Her heart-strings like to crack:
For, much she fear'd the grisly Ghost
Would leap upon her back.

Still on, pat, pat, the Goblin went,
As it had done before:
Her strength and resolution spent,
She fainted at the door.

Out came her husband, much surprised:
Out came her daughter dear:
Good-natur'd Soul ! all unadvis'd
Of what they had to fear.

The Candle's gleam pierc'd through the night,
Some short space o'er the green;
And there the little trotting Sprite
Distinctly might be seen.

An Ass's Foal had lost its Dam
Within the spacious Park;
And simple as the playful lamb,
Had follow'd in the dark.

No Goblin he, no imp of sin:
No crimes had ever known.
They took the shaggy stranger in,
And rear'd him as their own.

His little hoofs would rattle round
Upon the Cottage flooor;
The Matron learn'd to love the sound
That frightened her before.

A favourite the Ghost became;
And, 'twas his fate to thrive:
And long he lived and spread his fame,
And kept the joke alive.

For many a laugh went through the Vale;
And some conviction too . . .
Each thought some other Goblin tale,
Perhaps, was just as true.

Robert Bloomfield, Rural Tales, Ballads and Songs, *(1803), pp 70–77*

9 · RURAL RECREATIONS

William Kemp Dances Through Suffolk : 1600

William Kemp, who described himself as the 'Morris Man', accepted a wager to dance from London to Norwich in nine days. This he achieved, although the nine days were not consecutive. Here he relates his experiences in Suffolk, from Sudbury to Thetford.

In this towne of Sudbury, there came a lusty tall fellow, a butcher by his profession, that would in a Morrice keepe mee company to Bury: I being glad of his friendly offer, have him thankes, and forward we did set: but ere ever wee had measur'd halfe a mile of our way, he gave me over in the plain field protesting, that if he might get a 100 pound, he would not hold out with me; for indeed my pace in dauncing is not ordinary.

As he and I were parting, a lusty Country lasse being among the people, cal'd him faint-hearted lout: saying, 'If I had began to daunce, I would have held out one myle though it had cost me my life.' At which words many laughed. 'Nay' saith she, 'if the Dauncer will lend me a leash of his belles, Ile venter to treade one mile with him my selfe.' I lookt upon her, saw mirth in her eies, heard boldness in her words, and beheld her ready to tucke up her russet petticoate, I fitted her with bels: which she merrily taking, garnisht her thicke short legs, and with a smooth brow bad the Tabrer begin. The Drum strucke, forward marcht I with my merry Maide-marian: who shooke her fat sides: and footed it merrily to Melfoord, being a long myle. There parting with her, I gave her (besides ker skinfull of drinke) an English crowne to buy more drinke, for good wench she was in a pittious heate: my kindness she requited with dropping some dozen of short Courtsies, and bidding God blesse the Dauncer, I bade her adieu: and to give her her due, she had a good eare, daunst truly, and wee parted friendly. But ere I part with her, a good fellow my friend, having writ an odde Rime of her, I will make bold to set it downe.

> A Country Lasse browne as a berry,
> Blith of blee in heart as merry,
> Cheeks well fed and sides well larded,
> Every bone with fat flesh guarded,
> Meeting merry Kemp by chaunce
> Was Marrian in his Morrice daunce,
> Her stump legs with bels were garnisht,
> Her browne browes with sweating varnisht:
> Her browne hips when she was lag,
> To win her ground, went swig a swag,
> Which to see all that came after,
> Were repleate with mirthfull laughter.
> Yet she thumpt it on her way,
> With a sportly hey de gay,
> At a mile her daunce she ended,
> Kindly paide and well commended.

At Melford, divers Gentlemen met mee, who brought me to one Master Colts,[of Cavendish] a very kinde and worshipfull Gentleman, where I had unexpected entertainment till the Satterday. From whose house having hope somewhat to amend my way to Bury, I determined to goe by Clare, but I found it to be farther and fouler.

From Wednesday night til Satterday having bin very troublesome, but much more welcome to Master Colts: in the morning I tooke my leave, and was accompanied by many Gentlemen a myle of my way. Which myle Master Colts his foole would needs daunce with me, and had his desire, where leaving me, two fooles parted faire in a foule way: I keeping on my course to Clare, where I a while rested, and then cheerfully set forward to Bury.

Passing from Clare towards Bury, I was invited to the house of a very bountifull widow, whose husband during his life was a Yeoman of that Countrie, dying rich no doubt, as might well appeare, by the riches and plenty that abounded in every corner of the house. She is called the widow Everett. [of Hawkedon]

At her house were met above thirty Gentlemen, suche, and so plentifull variety of good fare, I have very sildome seene in any Commoners house. Her behaviour being very modest and friendly, argued her bringing up not to be rude. She was a woman of good presence: and if a foole may judge, of no small discretion.

From this widdowes I daunst to Bury, coming in on the Sat-terday in the afternoone, at what time the right Honorable the Lord Chief Justice entred at another gate of the towne, the wondring and regardless multitude making his honor cleere way, left the streets where he past to gape at me: the throng of them being so great, that poore Will Kempe was seaven times stayed ere hee could recover at his Inne. By reason of the great snow that then fell, I stayed at Bury from Satterday in the second week of my setting foorth, til Thursday night the next weeke following.

Upon Friday morning I set on towards Thetford, daunsing that tenne mile in three houres: for I left Bury somewhat after seaven in the morning, and was at Thetford somewhat after ten that same forenoone. But indeed considering how I had been booted the other journeys before, and that all this way or the most of it was over a heath, it was no great wonder: for I far'd like one that had escaped the stockes and tride the use of his legs to out-run the Constable: so light was my heeles, that I counted the ten miles no better than a leape.

Revd Alexander Dyce, Kemps nine daies wonder *(1840), Camden Society, pp. 9-12.*

Drawing Match at Needham Market : 1742

This is to give Notice to all manner of Persons, that on Wednesday the 19th of May, at the sign of the THREE TUNS in Needham Market, will be given gratis, a SILVER CUP of a guinea and a half value, to be drawn for by any five Horses, Mares, or Geldings, that make Twenty of the best and fairest Pulls, and carry the Weight over the Block with the fewest Lifters.

NB. No less than two Teams to draw for the aforesaid Cup.

At the same place on that Day will be given a PUNCH LADLE of fifteen Shillings value, to be drawn for by single Horses, Mares, or Geldings; which soever of the said Horses, Mares or Geldings, shall make Twenty of the best and fairest Pulls, according to the Judgement of proper Persons, shall be entitled to the Prize.

   NB. No less than five to draw for the said Ladle, and the Owner of each Horse, etc. to put down one shilling.
Ipswich Journal, 1 May 1742

Sir John Cullum gives this description of a drawing match:

The trial is made with a wagon loaded with sand, the wheels sunk a little into the ground, with blocks of wood laid before them to increase the difficulty. The first efforts are made with the reins fastened, as usual, to the collar; but the animals cannot, when so confined, put out their full strength; the reins are therefore afterwards thrown loose on their necks, when they can exert their utmost powers, which they usually do by falling on their knees, and drawing in that attitude. That they may not break their knees by his operation, the area on which they draw is strewn with soft sand.
Revd Sir John Cullum, History and Antiquities of Hawstead and Hardwick, *(1784), pp. 222-223*

Cock Fighting : 1749

THIS is to give notice. That on Monday next being the 13th of March, there will be a MAIN of COCKS shown in the Three Pigeons in Bury, between the Gentlemen of Norfolk and the Gentlemen of Suffolk, to show 15 Cocks on each Side, for Two Guineas a Battle and Five the odd battle. And on Tuesday the 14th Day, there will be a Pair of SILVER SPURS to be fought for in a Battle Royal, and no less than 13 Cocks to fight for the same; the Owner of each Cock to put in 2s 6d and that Cock that fights longest shall have the Spurs.
Ipswich Journal, 11 March 1749

Beccles Theatre : 1787

Saturday night last the New Theatre at Beccles was opened for the first time, when the comedy of 'The Suspicious Husband' with the musical farce of 'The Flitch of Bacon', was performed before a genteel audience. The theatre is a handsome brick edifice; and there seems little doubt but that the liberality of the inhabitants of the town and neighbourhood will make it fully answer the manager's expectations, whose principal aim seems to be that of furnishing them an agreeable evening's amusement.

Bury and Norwich Post, *6 June 1787.*

Pub Race : 1811

Yesterday se'nnight Martin Canham, a shoe-maker, of this town, undertook for a wager of one guinea, to run to every public-house or inn in this town (53 in number) and to drink thereat what he pleased, within the space of two hours, but which he performed with apparent ease in an hour and a quarter. Half a pint of beer was got ready for him at each house, of which he frequently only sipped – The sign of the Tollgate, near a mile from the town, was included.

Bury and Norwich Post, *13 November 1811.*

Camping

CAMP, an ancient athletic game at ball, now almost superseded by cricket, a less hardy and dangerous sport. Yet camping, though not so general, is still a favourite exercise in some districts of our county.
The late Right honourable William Wyndham... was wont to say, that it combined all athletic excellence; that to excel in it, a man must be a good boxer, runner and wrestler; in short, a sort of pancratiast. Certainly, no kind of manly exercise can display to so much advantage the powers, proportions, and attitudes of a fine muscular frame. The late Lord Rochford was also a great patron of this sport in the neighbourhood of his seat at Easton in Suffolk. Perhaps some varieties in the mode of playing it always existed; and certainly it is now

degenerated, and some meaner exercises unworthily usurp its name. Of the sport itself, however, two varieties are at present expressly recognized; rough-play, and civil-play. In the latter, there is no boxing.

But the following is a general description of it as it was of old, and in some places still continues. Two goals are pitched at the distance of 120 yards from each other. In a line with each are ranged the combatants; for such they truly are. The number on each side is equal; not always the same, but very commonly twelve . . . The ball is deposited exactly in the mid-way. The sign or word is given by an umpire. The two sides, as they are called, rush forward. The sturdiest and most active of each encounter those of the other.

The contest for the ball begins, and never ends without black eyes and bloody noses, broken heads or shins, and some serious mischiefs. If the ball can be carried, kicked, or thrown to one of the goals, in spite of all the resistance of the other party, it is reckoned for one towards the game; which has sometimes been known to last two or three hours. But the exertion and fatigue of this is excessive. So the victory is not always decided by number of points, but the game is placed against time, as the phrase is. It is common to limit it to half an hour; and most campers, have in that time got enough of so hardy a contest. The spirit of emulation prevails, not only between the adverse sides, but among individuals on the same side, who shall excel his fellows. The prizes are commonly hats, gloves, shoes or small sums of money.

Robert Forby, The Vocabulary of East Anglia, *vol i (1830), pp 50–53.*

Bell Ringing at Coddenham : 1740

This extract is included in memory of Ranald Clouston, Suffolks leading authority on bells, who died in March 2002. At the mention of a church Ranald could quote the number, tone, make and even the inscriptions on the bells. I was honoured to act as Bishop's Chaplain when the bell, in memory of his wife Kitty, was dedicated at Tostock in February 2000.

This is to give Notice, that on Wednesday the 31st Instant the New Peal of Bells at Coddenham, will be fit for Ringing for the first Time: And therefore all Lovers of that Science are desir'd to meet at the CROWN INN in Coddenham to hear them.

Our Subscribers desire the Society at Ipswich will give us the pleasure of their Company early to make a beginning.

All Gentlemen will be well entertain'd, and meet with a hearty Welcome from their humble Servant in Cornard GEORGE COOPER. Ipswich Journal, *27 December 1740.*

CODDENHAM S. Mary.   Tenor c. 15 cwt.   8 Bells.

1 Theodore Ecclestone,   Esqr, 1742. Thomas Lester made me.
  Although I am but small
  I will be heard above you all.

2 Thomas Lester made me 1742. The: Ecclestone.

3 Theodore Ecclestone.   Thomas Lester made us all, 1740.

7. Thomas Lester made us all 1740.

8. Thomas Lester of London made us all. 1742.

4 The Revd. John Longe, Vicar, John Fox, James Brook
  Church Wardens.
  Thomas Mears and Son of London fecit 1806.

5, 6 Recast by John Warner & Son, London, 1878.
  These bells are for the honour of God & the use of His Church
  Revd. Robert Longe, Vicar of Coddenham.
  Walter Chapman   } Church
  Frederick Gull   } Wardens.

Revd. John Raven, The Church Bells of Suffolk, *(1890), p. 178.*

Boxing Match at Onehouse : 1818

PITCHED BATTLE On Wednesday, about 10 o'clock in the forenoon, a grand boxing match took place in a meadow near the Shepherd and Dog, at Onehouse – between Burch of Finborough, a Wheelwright, and Balls of Buxhall, a husbandman, for £1 a side. Desperate and bloody was the conflict, which lasted for an hour and 10 minutes. The palm was at length awarded to Burch: but, so bruised and battered was the victor, that his life was despaired of. It did not appear that either of the 'artists' had been bred in the school of Mendoza, Crib, Scroggins, or any of the renowned heroes of the ring: for they displayed none of that profound science, a masterly manoeuvre, for which those distinguished personages are famed. On the contrary, all

that they achieved was the result of 'downright thumping'; by which, however, they had the felicity of affording infinite amusement to a vast concourse of neighbouring farmers assembled on the spot. Burch was light and nimble; but Balls was what the 'gemman of the fancy' term 'dead game'. In one respect, our 'Suffolk Heroes' were not behind their great prototypes of metropolitan celebrity. They had their regular seconds and bottleholders. Buckle, the painter, filled the former high and honourable office to Burch: and Catlin, of Finborough, to Balls. Messrs John Ward and George Maddison were the bottleholders. The quarrel we understand, which led to this 'empassioned strife', originated nearly a week before at Mr Rant's hop-picking. The cause, as usual, was 'one of the fair sex'; but, whether she were borne off in triumph by the victor, we have not heard. We presume this, however, to have been the case; as, with the characteristic generosity of Britons, a purse was made upon the ground , to soothe the wounded feelings of the loser!
Suffolk Chronicle, *30 October 1818.*

Horse Racing

Revd Isaac Taylor of Lavenham was a prolific author whose books included several moral and improving books for children. In this extract there can be no doubt of what he thought about gambling.

We have lately been at Norwich, where a great many poor people are working hard to get money, because they have but little: we are now come to Newmarket, where many rich people, who have got too much money, meet to squander it away in Horse-racing.

The horse is a noble animal; and when horses sport together in the field, kicking, and prancing in a variety of elegant attitudes, or racing against each other at their utmost speed, it is a very gratifying sight. But in this case they only continue it as long as they like, and leave off when they are tired. I like to see such a horse-race. It is quite a different thing, however, when the beautiful creatures are whipped and spurred beyond their fair strength, and forced to their utmost speed; for what? – that men may win a few guineas, by laying wagers (betting as it is called) on that which they think most likely to come first . . .
Revd Isaac Taylor, Scenes in England, *(1826), pp. 99–100.*

A Hasty and Rowdy Wedding : 1828

On the 8th inst. Mr James Burr, miller of Stanton, [was married] to Mrs. Sexton grocer and draper, of the same parish, and who had been a widow for the long period of eleven days. James Sexton (the former husband of the blooming bride) died on the 27th April; and it is reported that during the last three weeks of his illness, a match was agreed upon between his wife and Mr Burr; and further, that the wedding-cap and shroud were ordered at the same time – the cake for the funeral obsequies, and that for the solemnization of the matrimonial rites, manufactured in the same vessel! Whether this be true or not, it is certain that Sexton was buried on Friday the 2nd inst.; the next day the bans for the marriage of Mr. Burr and the Widow Sexton were entered in the book appointed for that purpose; but it was discovered on the Sunday that the Minister must have a week's notice of the intention of the parties. This was too long to wait; they therefore gave up their intention of being married in this round-about way, and off they hied to Bury to purchase a license.

On their return to Stanton, as many of the inhabitants were anxious that due honour should be done on the occasion, a great number of persons met Mr. Burr and the Widow at Ixworth; they here formed themselves into a regular procession to escort them home; a band of music was provided, composed of kettles, old boilers, and various other instruments, which vied with each other in the 'concord of sweet sounds', and 'ever and anon' a stream of light darted through the crowd in the darkness of the evening, produced by a sudden collision of a piece of steel with an old scythe. In this order, and amongst the most discordant sounds, Mr Burr and the Widow Sexton were marched into Stanton about 11 o'clock on Wednesday night, and after the band had paraded round the street several times, the crowd quietly dispersed towards their homes.

The next morning, however, it was understood that Mr Burr and the Widow Sexton intended to complete their agreement; the band again assembled, and the rough artisans of the village began to contrive various appropriate devices. A large white flag was attached to the house of the bride, and floated majestically across the street; an ass's skin, stretched upon a board as an emblem of the disgraceful nature of the marriage, and a white flag with a rude drawing of a coffin with the bride's former husband quietly deposited therein, were borne by two men, habituated in white shirts, black scarfs, and long white hat-bands. Others were dressed in garbs equally amusing, but black and white formed the principal part. The band of drums, kettles, rattles, &c. headed this procession, and they paraded the street all morning. An immense number of people had assembled, when, about 11 o'clock, the bride and bridegroom made their appearance, and lest they should be too roughly assailed, the constable undertook to conduct them safely to the Church: he walked before with his long staff of authority, then followed Mr Burr and the Widow Sexton, next the flags and music, playing 'Oh dear, what can the matter be!' and lastly the populace. In this order they were led to the very Church where, on the Friday previous, the widow had buried her husband; but, unfortunately, they then discovered that they had cone to the wrong Church, the license being for the other Church! However, that it might not be said that they had walked half a mile out of the way for nothing, the bride and bridegroom were made to pay a visit to the grave of old Sexton, and the question was put in due form whether he was willing that his widow should be joined in the bands of matrimony with James Burr; but Sexton answered not a word, and so some of the crowd in his name, gave consent. The procession now walked back to the other Church, where the ceremony was performed.

The Church and churchyard were crowded to excess, and the constable was obliged to stand at the altar with his staff, to keep off the pressure of the people and preserve order. When the ceremony was over, the music played 'Go to the Devil and shake yourself,' and the church-bells rang a merry tune. Mr and Mrs Burr repaired to the house of the latter to spend the remainder of the day, while the band, &c, parade the town till evening, when the musicians, flag-bearers, &c, resorted to the public-houses to spend the money they had obtained for their exertion in endeavouring to shame those in whom no shame existed. Night threw her sable mantle on the proceedings – the follies of the day ceased – and Stanton was itself again. There is no great disparity of years between Burr and his wife, but there are strong suspicions that the money which old Sexton had earned by his labour was the object of the marriage. His son, however, will not be deprived of his share, as Mrs Burr was cited into the Ecclesiastical Court, two days after her marriage, to compel her to administer. An inventory has in consequence been taken of the property, and Mr Burr will find that his golden vision will vanish, and leave him only the enjoyment of his wife.

Bury and Norwich Post, *21 May 1828*

Earl Soham Fair : c.1840

In the way of amusements, the great event of the year in our district was Soham Fair. The Races at Ipswich had not half as much attraction. The Fair was held at Earl Soham, in a large meadow close to a public-house. The ground was often filled, while the public-house invariably overflowed. The village presents no particular claims to attention, and one wonders how it ever obtained the privilege of having an annual fair, until one hears that a court favourite, Roger Bigod, procured it, in an age when a powerful Baron was as important as a King. It was a Lamb fair, and once a year, in the second week of July, the whole district was deranged by the vast flocks of lambs and sheep, which passed through the villages on the way to Soham Fair. Breeders from the sands, when feed became scarce in summer, sold their lambs to farmers in the clay district, who generally had plenty at that period. Soham being a convenient spot between the two districts, the Fair became the most attractive in the county, and a large amount of business was done.

Fifty years ago, after business was over, the farmers, and their daughters more particularly, entered into the delights of the 'pleasure' fair, and I have known several married couples of that class whose engagements began at the Fair. I went once. There were shows like Richardson's, or Samwell's, with dancing on a platform in front, a loud sounding and not over tuneful band, with a very big drum, and some over illustrated pictures of what was to be seen inside. Other shows had curiosities for rustics, such as a quiet young crocodile, monkeys, a serpent and a few snakes, giants, dwarfs, a fire-eater, knife swallower, and other marvellous attractions; clown and pantaloon, with coarse wit that passed current in the district for the years after; a theatrical performance, with a princess overpoweringly beautiful, and a villain outrageously murderous. But the most attractive play was the murder at the Red Barn, and this, I was told, had been so ever since the Polstead murder. There were also sparring booths, dancing booths (the latter much patronised), peep shows, swinging boats, roundabouts, and a lot of ginger-bread stalls. I remember seeing the forwards-famous Jem Mace, with his sparring dress on, seated in a drinking booth, feeding from a large plate of cold boiled beef and cucumber and onion with, say, a quarter-pint of vinegar to moisten the mass. He was a thick-set, brown, good-looking youth, and not thought much of as a fighter at the time. I think the charge for admission to the booth at which he assisted was a penny.

In early times, before the means of communication with towns was easy, these fairs afforded a convenient opportunity for friends to meet, and afterwards they made their yearly purchases. When I went to Soham Fair I saw a considerable quantity of woodware, earthenware, and iron goods displayed, and very little in the silk and calico line. It goes without saying that there were all sorts of 'playthings,' and the toy and gingerbread stalls did a thriving trade. The dancing booths were well patronised by farmer's sons and daughters. In fact, the first day of the fair was a time for a general merrymaking of all classes. The Rector of Monk Soham in those days – the father of the late Archdeacon Groome – was one of those jolly, good-humoured fellows who are fond of feasting their friends in princely style. At his dinner parties a bottle of port per man was the regulation allowance, but a double quantity was not forbidden. During the fair this Rector kept open house for the parsons, the country squires, and their wives and daughters, who flocked there at such times from all parts of the country for miles around.

John Glyde (ed), The Autobiography of a Suffolk Farm Labourer, *Suffolk* Mercury, *(1894 - 95).*

10 · CHURCH AND CHAPEL

Suffolk Churches

No one who essays to write on Suffolk can possible leave out the churches, for they are in a constellation that shines with unequalled splendour. They form the most picturesque and distinguished feature of the landscape to which they belong by virtue of material and genius. Nowhere else, unless it be in Norfolk, will you find such magnificent flowering, often in the most unlikely places. Cathedral-like in size and grandeur, they are tucked away in tiny hamlets and burst upon the view with a suddenness and wonder that one associates with the discoveries of an explorer. Embowered in trees, amid which one can detect them from a short distance but cannot reach by any apparent road, or standing sentinel amid their clustering cottages or situate in the precincts of a private park, they stand for all that is best of the countryside, silent memorials of a great art, expressed by long dead, loving and unknown hands. Many are thatched, appearing still in the coverings with which their builders crowned them. Some are tiled and others, the more wealthy, have coverings of lead. Not many have spires, although a few prink the sky in thin gracefulness.
Allan Jobson, North East Suffolk, *(1948), p. 40.*

The Commission of William Dowsing : 1643

William Dowsing was not the deranged iconoclast so often portrayed in church guide books. His commission or 'job description' shows exactly why and what he had to remove, in order to cleanse churches and chapels. His Journal records in detail what he did, or ordered to be done, in the churches he visited, although, as at Covehithe, he met resistance. In the extract 'superstitious' means asking for prayer for the dead.

HALESWORTH, April the 5th. 2 Crucifixes, 3 of the Holy Ghost, and a 3d of the Trinity altogether; and two hundred other superstitious Pictures and more; 5 popish Inscriptions of Brass, and the Steps to be levelled by the Parson of the town; and to take off a Cross on the Chancel. And then the Churchwardens had order to take down 2 Crosses off the Steeple.

REDISHAM MAGNA, April the 5th. A Crucifix, and 3 other superstitious Pictures; and gave order to Mr.Barenby,the Parson, to levell the Steps in the Chancel. He preach but once a Day.

RINGSFIELD, April the 5th. The Sun and Moon: and JESUS, in Capital Letters; and 2 Crosses on the Steeple: We gave order to take them down; and levell the Steps in 14 Days.

BECCLES, April the 6th. Jehovah's between Church and Chancel; and the Sun over it; and by the Altar, My Meat is Flesh indeed, and My Blood is Drink indeed. And 2 Crosses we gave order to take down, one was on the Porch; another on the Steeple; and many superstitious Pictures, about 40.—Six several Crosses, Christ's, Virgin Mary's, St. George's and 3 more; and 13 Crosses in all; and Jesus and Mary, in Letters; and the 12 Apostles.

ELLOUGH, April the 6th. We brake down 12 superstitious Pictures; and the Steps to be levelled; and a Cross to be taken off the Chancel, which they promised to do.

SOTTERLEY, There were divers superstitious Pictures painted, which they promised to take down; and I gave order to levell the Steps; and to break in pieces the Rails, which I have seen done; and to take off a Cross on the Church.

BENACRE, April the 6th. There was 6 superstitious Pictures, one Crucifix, and the Virgin Mary twice, with Christ in her arms, and Christ lying in the Manger, and the 3 Kings coming to Christ with their presents, and St. Catherine twice pictured; and the Priest of the Parish . . . O Christ govern me by thy Mother's Prayers! And 3 Bishops with their Mitres; and the Steps to be levelled within 6 weeks. And 18 JESUS's, written in Capital Letters on the Roof, which we gave order to do out; and the Story of Nebudchadnezzar; and orate pro animabus, in a Glass Window.

COVEHITHE, April the 6th. We brake down 200 Pictures; one Pope, with divers Cardinals, Christ and the Virgin Mary; a Picture of God the Father, and many other, which I remember not. There was 4 Steps with a Vault underneath, but the 2 first might be levelled, which we gave order to the Churchwardens to do. There was many inscriptions of JESUS in Capital Letters, on the Roof of the Church, and Cherubims with Crosses on their Breasts; and a Cross in the Chancel; all which with divers Pictures, in the Windows, which we could not reach, neither would they help us to raise the ladders; all which, we left a Warrant with the Constable to do, in 14 days.

Revd C. White, The Journal of William Dowsing, *(1885), pp. 6-7, 25-26.*

Social Control by the Church Court

The Archdeacon's Court could impose penance on anyone found guilty of a 'moral crime', who had been reported by the parish churchwardens. The public humiliation the penance enacted was designed both as an absolution and a preventative. If you are wondering about Ann Brown – she was allowed to do her penance in the Vestry or Parsonage House, in the presence of the Cleric and Churchwardens. The moral and message is – 'just say no!'

In the Court of the Worshipfull the Archdeacon of the Archdeaconry of Sudbury.

A schedule of Pennance Enjoyned the 29th Day of September 1759 by the Reverend John French Clerk M.A . . .

To Reuben How of Stanningfield in the County of Suffolk Singleman for the Crime of Fornication by him confessed to have been committed with Ann Brown of the same Parish Singlewoman. To be by him performed in the Parish Church of Stanningfield aforesaid on some Sunday before the last Day of October next ensuing.

First the said Reuben How at the Peal for Morning Prayer shall come into the Church porch of Stanningfield aforesaid and shall there stand until the second Lesson for Morning Prayer is ended arrayed in a White Sheet down to his feet with a white Wand in his hand and a paper Pinned to his Breast expressing his Offence, asking forgiveness of all that comes to Church.

Also the Second lesson being ended the Minister shall receive him into the Church and being Placed before the Desk with his face to the Congregation and Standing on a Pess [Kneeler] that he may be seen of all the People shall say after the Minister with an audible Voice as follows.

I Reuben How do confess and acknowledge that I have most greviously offended Almighty God and provoked his just Wrath and Indignation against me by committing the heinious Sin of Fornication with Ann Brown. I am heartily Sorry for this my Offence and Heinous Sin, and do from the bottom of my Heart repent of the same and do beg of God Mercy and forgiveness and do humbly Pray this Congregation here Present to accept of this my unfeigned Submission and Acknowledgment and to forgive the Scandal I have given to you all and to the Profession of Christianity. And I do Promise for the remainder of my life to live Soberly, chastely and Godly, which that I may do I desire you all Present to join with me in Prayer Saying – Our Father etc..

The Performance hereof is to be certified under the hands of the Minister & Churchwardens of Stanningfield aforesaid into the Registry of the Court on or before the 30th Day of October next Ensuing being Court Day.

Suffolk Record Office (Bury) E 14/7/12

William Pipe, Parish Clerk : 1823 – 1892

There have been many changes during seventy years, and when first appointed in succession to his father, he was doubtless a far greater man than he was at his death. Few of his class then could read, and he was truly the voice of the people, as he led them through prayer and psalm, speaking slowly, and in the Suffolk dialect which they all could follow. Now the responses are said by the choir, but there are a few old people, survivors of those unlettered days, who stand with vacant eyes and bookless hands, lost without a guiding voice they had learned so well to understand.

'The church will never feel itself without him', they say, and it certainly does not look itself. He made a picture sitting in his carved seat below the reading desk, a large prayer book open before him, and the light from a south window falling on his snowy hair and lion-like face, revered with age. When he stood he was taller than most of the congregation, and leaned forward his face lighted with pleasure, as his musical old voice started the chants and hymns.

It is sad to think how few of his friends are left to remember even fifty years ago; none can remember a time when he was not a clerk; he had but one contemporary – an old woman – and she outlived him by a few days. Yet though the people are changed, the village remains nearly as it was on that distant day when his mother carried him up to the quaint reed-thatched church to be christened. [1802]

The interior of the church has been altered even since the days of my grandmother. The high pews are gone, a vestry has been built out from the north door hiding a beautiful Norman arch, and the singing gallery has vanished. In it young Pipe used to lead the 'musick' of flutes and fiddles, ere he moved down to sit among the schoolboys, upon whose heads he wielded the actual staff of authority. The pulpit hath, saith tradition, been moved so often that an old churchwarden suggested that it should be furnished with wheels, so that the 'reverends' could place it where they pleased, without further expense to the parish . . .

Katherine Doughty (1892), in Allan Jobson, Victorian Suffolk (1972), pp. 131-32.

Divorce in Church : c.1840

At this period there was a curious custom in force, which to-day seems peculiar. Among poor people, the men sat on the right-hand side of the church and the women on the left. In parishes where a squire resided, he and his wife occupied a high-backed comfortable square pew, cushioned and carpeted. The low rush-bottomed chair was not then dreamed of, but for a labourer to sit alongside his wife in the house of prayer was, in clerical eyes, almost a crime. Even if a well-dressed man, a stranger, entered the church, and took his seat on the left-hand side, the clerk would send a lad to tell him, 'Please, sir, the women sit on this side.' If a labourer got married during the week, he was allowed to walk up to the 'altar' with his bride, and after the ceremony he marched down the aisle with his wife on his arm; but if he attended the church on the following Sunday, he was divorced from his wife as soon as he entered the porch. The service closed and he found himself in the churchyard before they were re-united.

John Glyde (ed), The Autobiography of a Suffolk Farm Labourer, Suffolk Mercury, (1894 – 95).

Revd John Ryle of Helmingham

John Ryle was the leading evangelical Anglican clergyman in mid Victorian Suffolk. He was Rector of Helmingham from 1884, appointed by the equally evangelical Tollemache family; Rector of Stradbrooke from 1861 and, in 1880 became the first Bishop of Liverpool.

We found the reverend gentleman preaching in a beautiful little Gothic church. He was surrounded by some of the finest statuary the county has to boast of – busts, effigies, and tablets; groups of mailed knights, mute representatives of a race of men long since passed away, have there a place. But this was not all, for a goodly number of devout worshippers were gathered there to listen to the deeply manly voice, and the fervent eloquence of the modern pastor. Although the population of the village is not more than 280, yet the congregation we found assembled, numbered something like 160, thus plainly showing that some of them must have come from the neighbouring villages. It was gratifying to observe that, although, in consequence of this fact, the number of those who are above the lowest ranks of society was greater then usual, the preacher never allowed the well-dressed element in his congregation to warp him from his own path, but, throughout the discourse, he spoke down to the understanding of the meanest one present, and every figure, every illustration was not only easy of comprehension, but was made interesting in itself from the facts of everyday life, or matters of local interest . . .

In addressing his village congregation, Mr. Ryle gives full scope to this faculty for illustration, and his discourse is consequently wonderfully picturesque, and very easy to remember . . .

We need hardly say that he preached extempore . . .

Speaking of the necessity of which the Christian was under of making himself thoroughly acquainted with the Bible, he observed 'Read your Bibles; do not depend alone upon what you hear from the pulpit. We may preach, lecture, write books and endeavour to teach, but we cannot make people read or study. We may lead a horse to water, but we cannot make him drink; we may set a feast before a man but we cannot make him eat . . .'

Again, after an anecdote from Bunyan, illustrative of the strange nature of the choice made by those who preferred the things of this life before the promises of God, the rev. gentleman observed: 'People will not accept that which is best; which is most enduring. What God promises endures through life; no man can deprive us of it. It endures through eternity – this cannot be said of the riches and the good things of this life. Will Sir William Middleton take Shrubland with him when he dies? Will the Earl of Stradbroke take Henham Hall when he dies? Will Mr. Austin take Brandeston Hall when he dies? Will Mr. Tollemache take Peckferton Castle or Helmingham Hall, or his fine house in St. James's, when he dies . . ?

'Silverpen' The Suffolk Pulpit, No. 19 in Suffolk Mercury March 1858.

High Church Innovations at Sudbury : 1865

The man responsible for the religious revival in Sudbury was Revd John Molyneux, Rector of Gregory and St. Peter (1855–79). The evangelicals and nonconformists thought him '. . next to Revd George Drury the most notorious man in the county for his Puseyism'.

I dined at a public-house in the market-place. The landlord having seated me in the bar parlour, filled up the intervals between the calls of the customers with talk, which seemed to ease his mind. 'The last five year,' he said, 'had worked a change in Sudbury: things was very different to what they used to be. Five year ago the young men was all for drink; now they was all for religion. There wasn't a quarter of the drink drinked now as there used to be. If 'twas a goin' to go on like that, keepin' a public-house wouldn't pay.' (He pronounced they and pay, as if spelt thy and py.) 'If so be there was ever another election, it 'ud be religion and not drink as 'ud carry the day. He couldn't think, for his part, what the pa'sons wanted. Look at the Peter church. Why, he had been told by them as hev been abroad as there ain't no difference between it and a Popish church. The pa'son wanted to try it on at the Gregory church; but the people wouldn't hev it, and a purty confusion the town hev been put to about the chairs. There was two hundred chairs, and the church wouldn't hev them.'

It was a question of chairs or pews to which he referred... I went to look at St. Peter's church,and found the door open. True enough: it did look very much like a Popish church, such as you may see in France. There are the same ornaments, the same fittings, the same clumsy ugly rush-seat chairs crowding the floor. From all that, it is but a short step to the images and the tawdry about the shrines. The 'Gregory church' perhaps foresaw danger in the two hundred chairs with which it was to be garnished.

Walter White, Eastern England, *(1865), vol. ii, pp. 195-196.*

Revd George Drury of Claydon

One of the most controversial figures of the Oxford Movement in the 19th century was the Revd George Drury, Rector of Claydon and Akenham from 1846 – 1895. The living belonged to his family and he in turn was both Rector and Patron. He embraced the principles of the Oxford Movement very early on and he furnished Claydon church in line with its ideals. Spurred on by his keenness to see the Monastic Life revived in the Church of England, he gave hospitality to Joseph Leycester Lyne (Father. Ignatius O.S.B.) and his handful of monks, who made their home at Claydon Rectory and who assisted in the parish from Shrove Tuesday 1863 until January 1864.

In the days when few clergy did so, Fr. Drury walked about his parish dressed in cassock and biretta and unashamedly used full Catholic ceremonial, including incense, in his church. An idea of the celebrations at Claydon during the period when Ignatius was 'assisting' him, may be seen from accounts of what took place on Ascension Day and St. Peter's Day 1863. On each occasion, the evening preceeding the festival saw a solemn procession from the

Rectory to a full church for a Vigil Service; then on the day itself a
Low Mass at 8.30 a.m., Morning Prayer at 10 a.m., a full Solemn
Mass at 11 a.m. and Solemn Evensong with Procession at 7 p.m. The
St. Peter's Day Mass included the Kyrie from Mendelssohn's Elijah
and the Sanctus and Gloria from Mozart's Second and Twelfth
Masses. The Evening Procession with acolytes, thurifer, servers,
choristers, monks and at least four banners, wound its way through
the streets of Claydon, headed by the crucifix, before returning to a
church bedecked in cloth of silver on its east wall, a cloth of gold altar
frontal and the cross and candlesticks upon the reredos wreathed in
summer flowers. Such awful disturbances followed this procession
that Ignatius was prevented from giving his prepared lecture about St.
Peter . . .

Shortly after Ignatius left for Norwich, Fr. Drury set up a
Benedictine Convent for women in a large house in the village street,
owned by a Miss Ware. This lasted until 1882 . . .

Then came the unfortunate incident in 1878, when Drury, obeying
the precepts of Canon Law, refused to read the Burial Service over the
unbaptised infant of a Baptist family at Akenham Church and had an
altercation with a Dissenting Minister who arrived to conduct a service
at the graveside. Drury felt that one of the newspapers had libelled him
and he sued the newspaper. Although he won his case, he was awarded
only 40 shillings. The Akenham Burial Case, was one of several
incidents which led to the Burial Laws Amendment Act of 1880.
Roy Tricker, Anglicans on High, (1988), pp. 30 & 40.

Sunday Services at Wetherden : 1887

It is a relief in these days of show, and noise, and motion, to
occasionally worship quietly in an old church, in an old-fashioned
way. Here were no white-robed choristers no choral service, no
resounding 'Glorias' and 'Amens,' no psalm chanting or elaborate
organ voluntaries. But a plain, quiet service, with canticles and hymns
sung, but all else read with a venerable clergyman, 86 years of age,
suitably clad in long flowing surplice, not wisped and crumpled, but
white like snow, and with broad folds such as a painter would like to
drape round his model; with no embroidered stole or narrow 'ribbon'

(such as the late Bishop of London called this adjunct), but with broad black soft-looking chaplain's scarf, and with Cambridge M. A. hood, worn in natural and in no eccentric copelike fashion. And in the pulpit the flowing Genevan black gown with long bands.

I have alluded to the great age of the minister, but to hear his clear sonorous voice, one would have cut down the years by half. The prayers were read, not intoned, or recited, or said, but read naturally, impressive and scholarly, and with such expression that one saw new points in almost every paragraph, and was more than ever struck with the sublimity of the English Liturgy. And the 'lessons' gave out new meanings through the lips of this venerable, godly, and scholarly minister of God; never have I heard them better read, naturally, but in no wise either flippantly or sensationally, but in a devout manner, with correct accent and emphasis, so that every word told. What a contrast to the drawling, singsong, and mouthing one often hears, in which the Word of God is desecrated, and is not 'understanded by the people.' And what of sermons? Half and three-quarters of an hour in length, preceded and followed by an extempore collect-like prayer; delivered extempore without note; earnest and solemn, with quaint, every-day illustration, and in the old Puritan style . . .

I could have wished to hear responses from the general congregation; my own voice, almost reduced to a whisper sounded to me strikingly loud in the Litany and Creed; a few spasmodic responses occasionally came from the singing seats at the west end of the church, but that was all; indeed the Incumbent apparently scarcely expected any responses, at any rate he did not wait long for any. Worthy man and venerable Divine, nearly last of his school, and almost a free historic survival, he worthily represents the old world traditions, and I doubt not is a faithful exponent of the Word, and a true minister of Jesus Christ . . .

Bury and Norwich Post, *19 July 1887.*

Methodist Preachers : c.1880

*Reuben Noy, of Westleton, was an agricultural labourer aged 80 in
1948, when Allan Jobson wrote down the memories of his long life.
Reuben was a life long Methodist and a Sunday School teacher for 60
years. Here he recalls Chapel events and preachers from his youth.*

'A rare lot o' folks came tew chapel when I wur young, whole families
on'em. They'd come in the morning tew the scule, bring thare dinner,
cook it up on the owd stove and stay all day, going home in the
darkness; fur thur wur ullus an arter meetin' an' thet didn't end till
drawin' on nine o'clock. Some o'them owd fellas cud whooly preach,
rare smiters they wur, an' they'd think nawthin' a walkin' fifteen miles
on a Sunday tew take a sarvice; Shank's nag thur and back. Come
Monday mornin' they git thare owd woman tew draw a needleful o'
worsted through thare blisters. Poor as poor cud be, but faithful, good
owd chaps wat wur the backbone o' nonconformist religion.'

'Owd Rowley Gissing wur a rare preacher, he cudn't read much nor
write, but his wife cud an' she helped him wi' his sarmons fur he had
a wunnerful memory and cud larn things off by heart. He had a shock
o' black hair and wud walk up an' down the rostrum passing his
hands through his raven locks an' whooly sweatin'. He had a
wunnerful sarmon about Elijah and the Prophets o' Baal, why even
the children ud sit an' listen an' never move.

'The Prophets called on thare god but thar wornt no answer; they
called again, but still no reply. 'Are yew asleep, partner?' 'Now,' say
Elijah, 'yew hev hed yare innings tewgither, now yew wait while I hev
mine!' He made the altar o' stoons, laid the fire an' put the sacrifice
on't, an' then he mad a deek [dike]an' filled thet wi' waater. When he
prayed, down come the owd fire, licked up the sticks, the stoons, the
waater, everything; thare worn't nawthin' left – nawthin"

'Whit-week wur the great time fur us; we used tew hev suffen on
narely the whool week. Tea an' meetin' at Yoxford, Monday:
Peasenhall, Tuesday; Middleton, Wednesday; Wenhaston, Thursday;
and sew on, an' we used tew gew tew the whool lot. Then we hed a
Fisherman's tea at Bilboro in January, an' a Sarvice o' Song
afterwards. We ullus used tew gew tew thet. '

'They wur great on Funeral Sarmons then, and it wur customary to
carry on the mournin' tew the next Sunday arter the buryin'. All the

mourners as cud ud come tew the sarvice, an' sit tewgither all dressed in black; praps a weepin' an' a takin' on kinder, an' the pracher ud let gew. In coorse yew know its wunnerful strange how good them folks be as die, an' yew can't allus fare tew recognise 'em when yew hares about 'em from the pulpit.

Allan Jobson, This Suffolk, *(1948), pp. 119–21.*

Church and Chapel at Akenfield

CHURCH

The parish church itself retains the mysterious quality of an ancient sacred place which has never been out of the possession of a long line of simple rural people. It is a steep, light building consisting of nave and chancel in one, an extravagant tower built of narrow orange-coloured bricks during the reign of Henry VII and a pinnacled Tudor porch. It stands near the foot of a hill to the north of the stream. The village once sat on the crests all around it, but for a hundred years since the draining of the valley more and more houses have appeared along the low road. The south side of the church is elaborate, decorated with flint cameos, stone carvings rich windows and intricate brickwork, and it also displays all the important tombs. The north side is an almost blank rubble wall looking much as the Norman/English left it. Paupers were buried behind it. Above the main churchyard, in an acre carved out of Accommodation Meadow, lie the recent dead under a harsh drift of stone-mason's chippings and white marble kerbs, crosses and books.

The interior of the church preserves the evidence of almost a millenium of national religious history. Two windows not much later than Domesday, stairs to the vanished rood, the Host and Mariolatry incised deep in the flushwork, decapitated evangelists huddled under the font, table silver (valued at £20,000 by Sotheby's) lent by a Renaissance squire for the altar after the King had taken the chalice, a table made for the divine Suppers of 1630, the mutilations of 1650, a great Jacobite bell named for Dr. Sacheverell, the pomp and Latin of the Augustans, an Oxford Movement reredos, Empire glory banners and now, on Laud's oak table, the flood of booklets about Vietnam, Marriage, Unity, the New English Bible and well-printed signs of expert publicist talents being employed to disseminate the new caritas. 'You must see our church,' they say in the village, ' it is pretty little place.' A long roster of servants arrange its flowers, polish its brasses, oil and wind the clock, tend the bells, hoover the carpets, launder the linen, mow the grass, heat, dust, trim. Gargoyles shoot the rain from the roof through screaming mouths. On its patronal day, the keys of St. Peter whip from the flagstaff, and in winter gulls sit in the louvres of the bell-chamber. The sea is near, yet, by Akenfield, quite unfelt. The tower is like a finger held up to test its existence. 'No, I've never been up it,' said the ditcher born in the village in 1908. 'I might'n fancy what I'd find.'

CHAPEL

The chapel is a pleasant square building made of red bricks and has a pyramidal 'Roman' or pantiled roof. There is a burial ground behind it. The windows have the blankness of an injured retina, a bloomy sightlessness. Texts in glass cases hang outside on the front wall and can be read by passengers in the village bus, which stops just there. Inside, there is a high rostrum for preaching, galleries and more texts. A trap-door in the centre of the large pale room covers a tank - the baptistry. The chapel says little – it doesn't intend to. It is no more than a sounding-box for all those describing the Word. Above it there is the spring from which the deacons, carrying pails on a shoulder harness, fetched water for the immersions before the mains were laid. By the side of it is the field in which their huge June rallies are held, in a tent which seats a thousand. It is a famous chapel and people once walked twenty miles to hear the Word in it.
Ronald Blythe, Akenfield, *(1969), pp. 59-60.*

An Anglo-Catholic Interior : Lound

The simple unprepossessing exterior of this small round-towered church on the Lothingland Peninsular gives little hint of the exquisite beauty and magnificence to be found inside it. People call it the 'Golden Church' and indeed its interior does shimmer with gold and many other fine colours. Here we have a splendid example of how the Anglo Catholic tradition, coupled with the skill of Sir Ninian Comper, can transform a small country church.

Lound is rich in elegant and beautiful woodwork, seen in its splendid openwork font-cover, grand organ-case and sumptuous Rood and rood-loft. Comper created here in 1914 something of what a mediaeval interior must have looked like before the Reformation. Our Lady, St. Salome and St. Elizabeth look out from their painted panels above the stone Lady Altar to the right of the screen. The sanctuary beyond shows so gloriously the beauty of Comper's work and his ability to create a superbly-proportioned, dignified and devotional setting for worship. The altar is furnished in the Sarum style, but with six candles. Its riddel-posts, crowned with golden angels, carry rich dossal curtains , where we see 'Comper Pink' predominating . . .

Here we see (and smell) the Catholic Tradition in all its richness and beauty, still working in a village church . . .

Roy Tricker, Anglicans on High, *(1988), p. 20.*

II · THE GENTRY

The Gentry of West Suffolk

Daniel Defoe here equates the houses and estates of West Suffolk, if not the climate, with those in France and Italy.

As I was pleasing myself with what was to be seen here, [Newmarket]I went in the intervals of the Sport to see the fine Seats of the Gentlemen in the neighbouring County, for this part of Suffolk, being an open champain Country, and a healthy Air, is form'd for Pleasure, and all kinds of Country Diversion; Nature, as it were, inviting the gentlemen to visit her, where she was fully prepar'd to receive them; in conformity to which kind Summons thy came; for the Country is, as it were, cover'd with fine Palaces of the Nobility, and pleasant Seats of the Gentlemen.

The Earl of Orford's House I have mention'd already, the next is Euston Hall, the Seat of the Duke of Grafton; it lies in the open Country towards the side of Norfolk, not far from Thetford; a Place capable of all that is pleasant and delightful in Nature, and improv'd by Art to every Extreme that Nature is able to produce.

From thence I went to Rushbrook, formerly the Seat of the Noble Family of Jermyns, lately Lord Dover, and now of the House of Davers.

After this we saw Brently, [Brent Eleigh] the Seat of the Earl of

Dysert, and the antient Palace [Brome] of my Lord Cornwallis, with several others of exquisite Situation, and adorn'd with the Beauties both of Art and Nature; so that I think, any Traveller from Abroad, who would desire to see how the English Gentry live, and what Pleasures they enjoy, should come into Suffolk and Cambridgeshire, and take but a light Circuit among the Country Seats of the Gentlemen on this side only, and they would be soon convinc'd, that not France, no not Italy itself, can out-do them, in Proportion to the Climate they lived in.

Daniel Defoe, A Tour Thro' The Whole Island of Great Britain, *(1724), p.77*

English Country Life

'What can you find to do in the country? Does not the time seem very long? Surely you must find it terribly slow!'

Such are the questions often put by the dwellers in towns to the dwellers in the country, and it is with polite incredulity that they receive the almost invariable answer, 'Oh, dear, no! the days are never half long enough for all we have to do.' Or perhaps the answer may be, 'Come and see.'

It was with some misgivings that we accepted an invitation to spend a week in a country house in Suffolk. Suffolk! The name suggested nothing but one large turnip-field! What had we ever heard of Suffolk? We searched our brains for every stray bit of information they could give us: agricultural depression loomed large in the foreground; impoverished landlords, ruined farmers, starving labourers—it did not sound cheerful! Was there nothing good that came out of Suffolk? We had heard of the Norfolk shooting, of the hunting in Leicestershire, but of Suffolk we could only remember that it was famous for a breed of chestnut cart-horses known as Suffolk punches, and for flocks of black-faced ewes called Suffolk blackfaces.

The train slows down, and we step out at the station of the little market town.

A tall broad-shouldered figure in tweeds, with 'country gentleman' writ large all over him, in his well-knit athletic frame and his easy, authoritative, and withal genial manner, steps forward to welcome us with cheery greeting and hearty English handclasp.

A respectful porter shoulders our portmanteau and gun-case, and we follow him to the high dogcart waiting outside the station. A smart groom is standing at the head of the handsome bay horse, and he touches his hat with a pleasant smile in sign of welcome. Already we begin to feel like coming home. We are soon bowling swiftly along the country roads, now at their best, since the dust of summer has been laid by September showers, and the winter stoning has not yet commenced, though the heaps in readiness by the roadside warn us of a via dolorosa to come.

The five miles between the station and the hall are covered almost too quickly by the trotting bay. We have so much to discuss by the way: the merits of the horses, and of other horses, individual and general; the cub-hunt to take place the next day; the prospect of continued fine weather; the shooting and the want of cover, and the wildness of the birds; things political, financial, and personal—till we turn in at the park gates, and a few minutes draw rein at the hall door.

The butler is apparently on the watch for us, for the door is flung open at once, and we enter to find a cheerful party assembled at afternoon tea in the entrance hall. This entrance hall is a beautiful old oak-panelled room, with the usual lounges and cushions, rugs and tiger-skins, table piled with litter of driving gloves, newspaper, hunting-crops, &c., portraits on the walls, and a bright fire blazing in the hearth, in front of which two or three of the family dogs have stretched themselves at ease . . .

The short October day is already closing in with the chill mists of evening, and the singing kettle, dancing firelight, and merry party in the comfortable hall all conspire to make as happy a haven as one could wish for at the end of a day's journey. We admire the dogs and see them perform their tricks, and make friends with the children before they are dismissed to their schoolroom tea.

When we retire to our room to wash off the dust of travel and change our things for dinner, we have the delightful sense of being quite at home. The butler, who in this house also performs the duty of valet, has already secured our keys, unpacked our portmanteau, set out the contents of the dressing-case, and laid out the clothes to be worn. He now appears with hot water, and to ask if we have any further need of his services.

Of late years, since the days of agricultural depression, which really do exist, the number of servants in country houses in this part of England has been much decreased. A butler, a footman, and perhaps six female servants, including the lady's maid, will now take the place of a former staff of a least a dozen. The lady of the house holds a position which is no sinecure when, as generally happens, she fills the post of house-keeper herself, and, with her small firm hand on the wheel, keeps the household machinery working smoothly and noiselessly, and yet never fails to 'come up smiling' from the midst of her cares and account books, to lay herself out for the entertainment and amusement of her gests. But the dinner-gong sounds, and we find our way down to the drawing-room.

The house-party is a small but pleasant one: two young sisters of our charming hostess and a cousin of our host home from India on leave. Conversation at table, consequently, is general and lively. The dinner is a simple one of three or four courses, well cooked and well served. The snowy damask, brilliant glass and old crested silver, softly shaded lamps and chrysanthemum-decked table, the pleasant babble of low-toned voices, and quiet movement of well-trained servants, make us feel how pleasant and restful a thing is a real English home.

We do not sit long over the wine before joining the ladies. The family portraits look down with wondering disdain to see their places taken by men who are contented with an extra glass of port, a cup of coffee with a liqueur, and an after-dinner cigarette, before making a move to the drawing-room. They were all two-bottle men themselves. Times have changed indeed since the days when it was the duty of one special footman to loosen the ties of the unconscious gentlemen under the table! In the drawing-room we have some music or a round game of cards; but the ladies soon retire, to be ready for an early start next day, and the men finish the evening with a long smoke in the billiard-room.

We begin to rearrange our views on the dullness of country life. Tennis is over with the summer, and regular hunting not yet begun, but the interim can be well filled with golf, shooting, and cubbing. There are two subscription packs of hounds within reach, with a modest 'cap' of five shillings – that is to say, the hat is sent round for a five-shilling subscription from non-subscribers. Annual sub-scriptions range from one guinea up to fifty pounds. The farmers are not expected to subscribe, though some of them do so. But in allowing the hunt to gallop over their land and break down their fences, in 'walking' puppies and 'squaring' keepers and fowl-owners, those who are interested in the sport are some of the hunt's best friends.

The country is not big, but awkward, with mud banks to the ditches and thick hedges. The ditches are still very 'blind,' as there have been no frosts to fetch the leaves off the overhanging bushes. A clever horse is wanted here more than a fast one, and bone and muscle, for the soil is stiff in the wet season.

Our host has offered us a mount for the next day, which we gladly accept. The meet is not till nine o'clock, instead of half-past five, as earlier in the season, and there is no particular hardship in getting down to breakfast at eight; so we take our candle and nod 'good-night,' with a pleased anticipation of the morning's ride.

At 7.30 the same imperturbable treasure of a man brings our shaving water, prepares our morning tub (hot or cold according to choice), lays out our riding suit and retires, presumably to see that breakfast is in course of preparation, or perform like services for others.

Those of us who are going to ride or cycle to the meet hurry gaily through breakfast – always an informal meal, which we take as we are ready for it.

As the horses are led round to the front door, we empty our cup of coffee or toss off a glass of sloe gin, button on our gloves, and hasten out, each eager to be the one to put up the ladies and settle their skirts for them. This privilege secured, we light our cigars, mount our impatient hunters, and wave our hats to the rest of the party and the children, who have just come down in time to see the start.

Half-past eight on a fine autumn morning in Suffolk! The dew still lies heavy on the grass by the roadsides, and the sun shines in long shafts of light through the silvery mist that hangs like white veil over the fields and woods.

The horses are as fresh as paint, and we trot gaily along, warming the chill out of our blood, and sniffing the cool damp air, laden with the fragrant scent of wet and dying leaves.

'Biota', The Eastern Counties Magazine, (1901–2), pp 173-79.

A Problem with Dialect

Lord Huntingfield, who lived at Heveningham, was desirous of making the acquaintance of Sir Philip Broke, son of the distinguished hero of *Shannon* and *Chesapeake* fame. Neither the baronet nor his lordship had seen each other, and therefore was unacquainted with any of those distinguishing marks by which one man knows his friend from his foe. An invitation to visit from the lord to the baronet was duly accepted, and on a stated day the latter ordered Woodrow his coachman, to drive him to the mansion of Lord Huntingfield. The Jehu, however, was puzzled by not seeing direction posts, and in traversing the dirty lanes and miry roads asked his way when he feared he was at fault. He spoke broad Suffolk, and in so doing sunk the euphonious length of the name attached to his lordship's mansion, and continued to ask which way to H'enham Hall, to Henham he was directed, and at the seat of Earl Stradbroke the baronet at length arrived.

Believing that Hevingham had been reached, he descended from his vehicle, and entered the princely mansion. His lordship is 'a-field', ejaculated the stately footman, but he expects a gentleman to dinner and will return shortly. The baronet was shown into a dressing-room, and having thoroughly equipped himself, descended in due time to the dining-room, and there, as he supposed, stood his noble friend. But, strange to say, amazement instead of welcome spread itself over the features of the owner of Henham, and at length came the hesitant enquiry, 'Why, who are you?' 'Me!' was the answer. 'Why, who are you—are you not Lord Huntingfield?' 'That I've been hunting and a-field all day,' exclaimed his lordship, 'I'll admit, sir; but I am Earl Stradbroke.' Some minutes elapsed before the real state of the case could be explained, and the awkward dilemma was overcome by the baronet remaining for the night under the hospitable roof at Henham, and the despatch of a courier to Heveningham Hall to tell the singular tale, and account for the non-appearance of the expected visitor.
Suffolk Mercury, *15 June 1894*.

Maharajah Duleep Singh

*The Maharajah was the last ruler of the Punjab and owner of the Koh-
i-Nor diamond. He was brought to England in 1854, aged 15 and
became a favourite of Queen Victoria. In 1863 he purchased the
Elveden Estate, modelling its Hall on an 'Indian Palace'. His grave is
a place of pilgrimage for Sikhs from all over the world.*

During this period H.H. the Maharajah Duleep Singh lived at Elveden
Hall and owned the Elveden Estate. His trustees purchased the Estate
from the executors of the late Mr. William Newton in 1863.
Subsequently he acquired the parish of Eriswell, adjoining. At
Christmas time a pair of rabbits would be sent to each household and
were considered a great treat. Another notable event would be a party
and sports held at Chamberlain's Hall Barn, Eriswell. The great barn
was warmed by turf fires on the earthen floor. I can recall seeing H.H.
the Maharajah, H.H.the Maharanee, and their two sons, the Princes
Victor and Frederick Duleep Singh, at one of these frolics. His
Highness, of medium height and powerful build, with side whiskers
and moustache, laughed heartily at the unsuccessful attempts to climb
the greasy pole, at the top of which a sovereign had been placed. The
Maharanee was an Egyptian lady. The two princes at that time had
long black hair.

I well remember seeing the Maharajah Duleep Singh partridge-
shooting on the three-cornered field that runs to the left from the
Eriswell crossroads to the blacksmith's shop at the beginning of
Eriswell village. It was in 1875 and I was a small boy of seven. These
were the days of muzzle-loaders and the Maharajah had three double-
barrelled guns, and two loaders, who with their blue and green coats
and waistcoats, powder flasks and leather shotbags, made a great
impression on my mind . . .

Both Prince Victor and Prince Freddy Duleep Singh were amazingly
quick shots; Prince Victor was always rated amongst the very highest,
though I should not have thought there was a great difference between
them. I should not place either in the top class for grace and style
alone, their build did not assist them in this, being of the short stocky
type and carrying a considerable amount of flesh, particularly Prince
Victor. All the same, from the killing point of view they needed a lot
of beating.

The Maharajah also was considered one of the best, but I was too young to be able to really appreciate first-class shooting when he was at his zenith . . .

T. W. *Turner,* Memoirs of a Gamekeeper, *(1954), pp. 20 & 84.*

Madam at the Hall

As this is written by Lady Cranworth, it is probable that this description is based on Grundisburgh Hall and village.

MADAM was a dear old lady, and the Hall was a most delightful house.

It is my home now, as it was hers years ago, and the village where she worked is the village where I live. But it is all so different from what it was one hundred years ago! The children whom madam taught, and petted, and scolded, are the old men and women of to-day, who are passing from us one by one. They talk about her with tears in their eyes, and little by little her picturesque individuality has taken form, till it seems to me to pervade the whole place.

The Hall where she lived her life, and which is the frame to her picture, is a very comfortable house. It was built in the days when the old Elizabethan houses were thrown down, and square ones were built in their stead...

Madam was a very pretty old lady with snow-white hair, which was done in two rolls on each side of her face, and a white cap which was tied under her chin. She was a small woman, but withal plump and comely, stately in spite of her inches, and commanding the willing respect of her daughters-in-law. She ruled her house well and wisely, and she governed all with whom she came in contact with a rod of iron. She was such a great lady, that the idea, never crossed her mind that anyone could oppose her will, and as a matter of fact no one ever did. 'She wur a rare masterful old lady, and although we all loved her right well, we feared her too! The Squire, he might rule his farms and his farmers, but she ruled her house and her village. Times are altered now, and folks would not stand it; but there they had to, and it wur a sight better for them. I'm thinking Madam was very particular about her cottages, and if anything went wrong in them there was a business! They had just to walk up to the Hall, and beg Madam's pardon humbly, or out they might go. Folks were much rougher in those days, and if there had been no check, it would have been very bad for the place . . .'

When Madam went to see the farmer's wives she was always dressed with sober richness. She wore rich black satin, unless it was velvet. She had a beautiful black velvet which opened down the back, and had two breadths of silk let in, so that when she sat down she pulled her dress apart, and did not sit upon the velvet.

She always tried to interest her tenants' wives about the farming. One of them said to her, 'But I know nothing about farm work.' To which Madam answered as quick as a thought: 'Then why don't you learn? When they are draining, as they are at present, go and see how the pipes are set.' She also tried to interest them in the poor about them . . .

But to turn to the dear old lady in her own home, which she ruled as despotically as she did her village. She not only kept her men-servants in livery, but she also expected her maidservants to wear it.

As the old keeper expressed it, 'The cook and the lady's-maid dressed private,' but all the undermaids wore neat lilac prints in the morning, and dark blue merino gowns in the afternoon, with round frilled caps which tied under their chins. Thy were all expected to attend church in a body, the menservants wearing their full dress livery of dark blue, with yellow collars.

Madam had a little old-fashioned pony carriage in which she drove about her village, but when she took her more formal airings she went in a yellow coach, drawn frequently by four horses, and driven by an old coachman, who was a devoted adherent of the family, and had their interests thoroughly at heart . . .

Among the other exemplary things which Madam did was to order the village up to the Hall at stated periods to be vaccinated. They all had to attend, whether they liked it or not, and Madam was present while the vaccination was done. The old keeper said he was nine years old when Madam first caused him to be vaccinated, and he was so much alarmed that he fainted right away at her feet. She and her maid brought him round again, and 'he minded right well that the medicine she gave him when he come to; that' (smacking his lips) 'wur not nasty, that wurn't.'

Every week Madam gave away soup, and she made a great point of being present when it was served out, that as the parishioners express it, 'she might see with her own eyes as cook did not favour one on us more than another, but as the bits o' mate were shared out fair. Indeed, whiles, she would ladle it out herself.'

At Christmas she asked all her school to a grand dinner in the servant's hall, and 'we did count on that! There were great large joints of beef smoking hot, and puddens, and puddens full of plums, all black wi' richness. Madam, she would come and see us eat it, and she made a point of our eating a lot. But after that she would say, 'Now yeo may eat the rest, or yeo may take it home.' That was so that our mothers might get a bit too; and most of us took some. That Christmas dinner was all the mate many of us saw in the year.'

Madam used to place out all her schoolgirls, of course, and one tale of her is very characteristic.

'Madam got Cassandra a place at a farmer's in t'next village. But it was a roughish place, though a good one, and the mawther was home-sick. The farmer's wife was a strict one, and, to make matters short, the girl come home! Well, her mother was real frightened, and took her up to Madam at once to ask what was to be done, and if the girl might bide at home.

'But Madam, she said no! she had found t'girl a good place, and there t'girl must bide; but go you home, she say, and I'll be a-thinking what I can do to help ye; so she thought; but she did nothing that week nor the next. And at the end o' that time she ordered out her coach and her two footmen, wi' their yellow and blue livery, and her shining horses, and she drove down in state to see that farmer's wife. She sent I for her to come and speak to her, and say she, very grand like, 'I ha' come to ask after the girl Cassandra. I take a great interest in her,' she say; and when the farmer's wife saw what great friends Cassandra had, she wur right good to her and helped her much.'

Lady Emily Frances Cranworth, The Eastern Counties Magazine, *(1900–1),* *vol.i, pp. 272, 276-83.*

12 · CRIME AND PUNISHMENT

Rules of Mildenhall House of Correction : 1668

Houses of Correction in the seventeenth century were exactly that – a place for 'short, sharp, shock treatment.' The weekly routine consisted of work, worship and whipping. If you were into the latter, this was the place to be!

Orders prescribed by the Justices to be observed by the keeper of the house of Correction in Mildenhall parish.

Imprimis [firstly] it is ordered that the said Keeper (or some one for him) doe everie day in the weeke morning and eveninge call all his prisoners together and then Reverantly Read some prayers out of the books of Common prayer and some part of scripture out of the new Testament or some psalms of David upon payne to forfeite everie such neglect 12d to be defaulted out of his wages.

2lie. That everie Lords day he doe bring all his prisoners to the Church morninge and evening and there place them in Seats built for them. Reverently to heare divine service sermon and Catechisinge and to examine them what they have learned, as also everie Saterday night and everie Sabboth morninge and eveninge to teach his prisoners to answer questions in a short Catechisme called Perkins Catechisme upon payne to forfeit 12d as aforesaid.

3lie. That upon the Cominge in of any prisoners the said keeper doth strip the body of the said prisoner from the Wast upward and give him or her Tenn Lashes with a whipcord Whipp until his or her body be blouddy.

4lie. That the said Keeper doe everie Friday Morninge Correct his said prisoners giving every on of them Fyve Lashes as aforesaid except such as are committed for A yeare and those only but three lashes.

5lie. That the said keeper upon the Releasinge of any prisoner doe give him, or her Tenn Lashes as aforesaid.

6. That the said keeper shall sett his prisoners to Worke and Correct such as will not Worke or be disordered or nastie.

7. That the said keeper shall well and truly pay unto every of his prisoners either in victual or money soe much as they shall earne by their Worke.

Suffolk Quarter Sessions Book, *Suffolk Record Office (Ipswich) B 159/2/7 f. 69.*

Highway Robbery at Great Barton : 1794

Saturday evening, between seven and eight o'clock, as Samuel Russell, commonly called the Botesdale Post, was returning home from this place, he was attacked near the two mile stone by two footpads, armed with bludgeons, one of whom aimed a blow at him across the head, but which fell on his shoulder, and the other struck him across the knee, and then demanded his watch and money, which they forced from him, amounting to about 5s in silver, and a quantity of halfpence, together with a number of small bills and receipts, and a penknife. On his hesitating to part with his watch and money, one of them swore most desperately, and desired the other to knock him down at once, and drag him out of the road. They looked into the box of the cart, in which his parcels are kept, but one said, let those things alone as they may lead to a discovery. One was a tall stout man, with a slop frock on, and the other a tall thin man, in a loose great-coat.

Bury and Norwich Post, *24 December 1794.*

Smuggling at Kettleburgh : 1784

Sunday last, about two o'clock in the afternoon, a seizure of 57 half-ankers of rum spirits was made at Kettleburgh in this county, by Messrs Bell and Pope, supervisors, and Messrs Engall, Mason and Spilling, excise-officers, with seven assistants. The same day, about four in the afternoon, as they were conveying these goods to Woodbridge, they were overtaken, near Easton, by a gang of villains, about 30 in number (all apparently stripped to thir shirts, except one) who, with horrid imprecations and expressions of Murder! Murder! fell upon them in a most inhuman manner, with an intent to rescue the seizure: however, the officers made a noble stand, and a bloody engagement ensued, which lasted near an hour, when the officers put the smugglers to flight, pursued them several miles, and maintained the seizure. Almost all the smugglers were wounded, and many of them very desperately; five or six of the officer's party were armed with carbines, pistols, and broad-swords. It is supposed the noted George Cullum, of Brandeston, was at the head of this banditti.
Ipswich Journal, 22 May 1784.

Wreckers on the Suffolk Coast

Where are the swains, who, daily labour done,
With rural games play'd down the setting sun;
Who struck with matchless force the bounding ball,
Or made the pond'rous quoit obliquely fall;
While some huge Ajax, terrible and strong,
Engaged some artful stripling of the throng,
And fell beneath him, foil'd, while far around
Hoarse triumph rose, and rocks return'd the sound?
Where now are these? – Beneath yon cliff face they stand,
To show the frightened pinnace where to land;
To load the ready steed with guilty haste,
To fly in terror o'er the pathless waste,
Or,when detected, in their straggling course,
To foil their foes by cunning or by force;
Or, yielding part (which equal knaves demand),

To gain a lawless passport through the land.
Here, wand'ring long, amid these frowning fields.
I sought the simple life that Nature yields;
Rapine and Wrong and Fear usurp'd her place,
And a bold, artful, surly, savage race;
Who, only skill'd to take the finny tribe,
The yearly dinner, or septenniel bribe,
Wait on the shore, and, as the waves run high,
On the tost vessel bend their eager eye,
Which to their coast directs its vent'rous way;
Theirs, or the ocean's, miserable prey.
*Revd, George Crabbe, 'The Village' (1783), George Crabbe, The Poetical Works
of Rev. George Crabbe (1840) vol. ii p. 78.*

The Murder of Maria Marten by W. Corder

*William Corder, Maria Marten and the Red Barn, were as well known
in Victorian England as Jack the Ripper and his victims. The story had
every aspect of a Victorian melodrama – romance, murder, the escape,
supernatural dreams, the arrest, trial and execution. Moyses Hall
Museum in Bury has William's death mask, his scalp and a book
covered in his skin and the knives and pistol used to murder Maria.*

Come all you thoughtless young men,
a warning take by me,
And think upon my unhappy fate,
to be hanged upon a tree;
My name is William Corder,
to you I do declare,
I courted Maria Marten,
most beautiful and fair.
I promised I would marry her
upon a certain day,
Instead of that, I was resolved
to take her life away.
I went into her father's house
the 18th day of May,
Saying, my dear Maria,

we will fix the wedding day.
If you will meet me at the Red-barn,
as sure as I have life,
I will take you to Ipswich town,
and there make you my wife;
I then went home and fetched my gun,
my pickaxe and my spade,
I went into the Red-barn,
and there I dug her grave.
With heart so light, she thought no harm,
to meet him she did go,
He murdered her all in the barn,
and laid her body low:
After the horrible deed was done,
she lay weltering in her gore,
Her bleeding mangled body
he buried beneath the Red-barn floor.
Now all things being silent,
her spirit could not rest,
She appeared unto her mother,
who suckled her at her breast;
For many a long month or more,
her mind being sore oppress'd
Neither day nor night
she could not take any rest.
Her mother's mind being so disturbed,
she dreamt three nights o'er
Her daughter she lay murdered
beneath the Red-barn floor;
She sent the father to the barn,
when he the ground did thrust,
And there he found his daughter
mingling with the dust.
My trial is hard, I could not stand
most woeful was the sight,
When her jaw-bone was brought to prove,
which pierced my heart quite;
Her aged father standing by

likewise his loving wife,
And in her grief her hair she tore,
she scarcely could keep life.
Adieu, adieu, my loving friends,
my glass is almost run,
On Monday next will be my last,
when I am to be hang'd;
So you, young men, who do pass by,
with pity look on me,
For murdering Maria Marten,
I was hang'd upon the tree.

James Catnach, 1828, Life and Times of James Catnach, (1878) p. 187.

Machine Breaking at Gosbeck : 1815

The introduction of threshing machines led to a series of rural uprisings 1815 – 43. The Gosbeck riot took place in a time of rural distress following the end of the Napoleonic Wars. The sentences were surprisingly light, as Transportation could have been the verdict.

A short time before I left school one of those extraordinary events occurred in Gosbeck which make villages notorious and provide food for gossip for many years after. There was a labourer's riot, and two threshing machines were destroyed. The marvellous fall in the price of corn and the alarming increase of the Poor-rate caused farmers to strain every nerve to reduce their weekly expenditure... Farm labourers suffered severely in the winter of 1815, and the introduction of machinery lessened their scanty means and added greatly to their distress. Children too young for work cried aloud for bread.

When two of the farmers, Mr. Nathaniel Baskett and Mr. Jonathan Beard, told the labourers that they could do without them, as they intended to use machines for threshing, the men became desperate, and resolved to make war on the instruments which robbed them of daily labour and their children of bread. We know now that the employment of machines brings about cheaper produce, but whilst the transition was going on, the labourers, whether in factory or in field, had to endure the severest privations. True, indeed is the proverb, 'Whilst the grass grows the horse starves.' It is not for me to dispute the wisdom of employing machinery. It is, however, none the less hard, when flesh and blood are driven out by cogs and screws.

The riot occurred one rafty morning, about ten o'clock, towards the end of February, 1815. It began at Mr. Baskett's. He lived in a farm at Crowfield, nearly opposite the 'Rose,' and his Gosbeck farm, where the threatened machine was kept, was worked off-hand. Where the crowd assembled I don't recollect, but plenty of gawky lads and swobbling women joined the throng as it marched to the scene of action. The ringleaders, fierce with excitement and anger, were armed with wooden beetles, and such axes as are used for felling trees. As soon as they got to the spot the storm broke. The hootings rose and filled the air, and William Ellis, the most rumbustical of the leaders, raised his heavy beetle and disabled the machine at the first blow. John Fenn, a couch-handed man, who was a frowsy looking customer, followed suit, and after cuffs and cuts from various men, the machine was left useless, amidst the clamour of voices and a roar which seemed ominous. This farm of Mr. Baskett's was on the turnpike road, but another machine was at Mr. Beard's, whose farm, though only a short distance off, was down a bye-road leading to Pettaugh. Amidst great noise and confusion this second machine was smashed, and the men threatened further mischief. But by this time, three or four constables, backed by one magistrate, and a body of farmers on horse and foot, made their appearance, and the ringleaders were at once taken into custody. Nine men were conveyed to Ipswich gaol; two of them found bail at once; the other lay in prison until the following Tuesday, when they were all committed for trial, but allowed bail. At the Assizes they were convicted, and each of them was sentenced to a month's imprisonment.

Imagine what their wives and children had to suffer while the husbands lay in prison. Great efforts were made to relieve them, but many of those who helped were nearly as poor as themselves. They, however, did their best, and even more than they were able. What would the poor do, were it not for the poor? At the expiration of their punishment the men returned to Gosbeck, obtained employment close at hand, and with one exception lived in the parish for many years.

John Glyde (ed), The Autobiography of a Suffolk Farm Labourer, Suffolk Mercury, (1894–95).

The Trial and Escape of Leach Borley : 1844

Leach Borley was one of the arsonists involved in this later period of discontent. He slipped his shackles and escaped custody at Bury Jail. Leach or 'Painter', was known as a fast runner and jumper! His swift escape and disappearance was commemorated in ballads, a version of which is still known in 'pubs and places where they sing' today.

BURY LENT ASSIZES: FIRE AT RYMER POINT. Leach Borley, aged 27, labourer, of Sapiston, was charged with having, on the 19th of November last, feloniously set fire to a barley stack in Troston, the property of Mr. George Gayford, of Rymer-house.

[After hearing all the evidence, the jury returned a verdict of guilty]

The learned Judge, in passing sentence, remarked that the prisoner had been found guilty upon evidence so clear as not to admit even of a doubt; and most certainly if the law had not been altered, he would have had to suffer death, for his crime. There appeared to be some motives of revenge against the prosecutor by the expression of the prisoner, and he had exercised a malicious and malevolent spirit by the destruction of the property, which injured not only himself but others also. By destroying that stack there was the loss of labour which would have been required to thrash it out; and where the owner of such property was a poor man, he became unable to find employment for his labourers. It was necessary, therefore that the strong hand of the law should protect such property, and he felt it to be his duty to carry that law out to its fullest extent, by sentencing the prisoner to be transported for life.

The prisoner exclaimed, on leaving the bar – 'I wish God may strike me for a corpse this minute, if I know anything about the fire!'

[On arrival at Bury Gaol Leach escaped from custody]

ESCAPE OF A CONVICT INCENDIARY – It will be seen by the report of our Assizes, that Leach Borley – (or, as he is better known in the neighbourhood of his crimes, 'Painter Borley') – was convicted, upon the clearest evidence, of having set fire to the stacks of Mr. George Gayford, at Rymer, between this town and Thetford. We lament to state, however, that on his return to the gaol, when he alighted at the prison door, he had succeeded in relieving himself from the irons by which he had been fastened to the other prisoners, having a very small hand, and throwing off his shoes, he bolted off between the officers in attendance. A pursuit was immediately made after him, but being remarkably swift, he was soon out of reach, having tripped up the heels of a man who attempted to stop him on Rougham Hill, and has not since been heard of. A description of his person will be found in an advertisement offering a handsome reward for his apprehension. Borley has long been notorious as a most daring offender. Previous to this offence he had absconded to avoid a warrant for breaking into a house to rescue a prisoner: he is also known to have shot a colt belonging to Mr. Kersey Cooper, steward to the Duke of Grafton; and these are but a small portion of his delinquencies. We trust he will not long remain undiscovered.

GAOL; BURY ST EDMUND'S,   April 5, 1844 : 25 GUINEAS REWARD; escaped. From the Gaol Van, in being conveyed from the Hall to the Gaol, about half-past Eight this Evening, LEACH BORLEY, commonly called PAINTER BORLEY, aged 27, 5 feet 7 inches high, light complexion, brown hair, grey eyes, rather long visage, small scar near the right eye, and marks near the left eye, received, it is supposed, from fighting, which he is fond of talking about, hands injured about the thumbs and knuckles from fighting; he also boasts of being a fast runner and jumper.

  Whoever will apprehend him and lodge him in Custody, shall receive the above Reward, by applying to Mr. Orridge, the Governor of the Gaol.

[He was never captured or heard of again. The following ballad 'celebrated' his escape]

Prisoner's Escape from the Gaol of Bury St Edmund's
At the Lent Assizes, 1844.

Good people listen unto me and a tale I'll relate,
Of a prisoner that stood at the bar his trial for to take;
His trial he did take as you may under stand,
He for life to be transport'd was unto some foreign land.

Then he with other prisoners were iron'd side by side.
Into the van then they did get unto the gaol to ride,
But when he descended from the van oh! he was so polite,
He left them all respectfully he wish'd them all good night.

Then about the town of Bury so quick they spread the news,
That Painter he had cut the stick and behind him left his shoes,
The rivers they were not so wide nor the gates were not so high,
For like a buck poor Painter over all them he did fly.

Then its early the next morning the news was spread abroad,
And five and twenty guineas it was the full reward,
There was five and twenty guineas in printed bills so plain,
For those that would bring Painter back to Bury goal again.

They have search'd the country for him they search'd it up and down,
They have search'd through every village likewise through every town,
They are eager for to catch him this praise then for to gain,
For they long to get him sailing upon the watery main

He is an active young man it's known to be true
He done his work so clever when he bid them all adieu,
Then a proclamation from the queen there surely ought to be,
Publish'd in the papers for to set poor Painter free.
Bury and Norwich Post, *10 April 1844; and Suffolk Record Office (Bury)
1557/6/17.*

I3 · COMMUNICATIONS

Suffolk Miles

Thence I went to Woodbridge 7 mile, mostly lanes enclosed countrys; this is a little Market town but has a great meeting for the Dessenters; hence to Wickham 5 mile more – but these are all very Long miles.

Thence to Saxmunday [Saxmundham] 8 miles more, this is a pretty bigg market town, the wayes are pretty deep, mostly lanes very little commons; I pass'd by severall Gentlemen's seats . . . generally the people here are able to give so bad a direction that passengers are at a loss at what aime to take, they know scarce three mile from their home, and meete them where you will, enquire how farre to such a place, they mind not where they are then but tell you so farre which is the distance from their own houses to that place; I saw at a distance as I descended some of their hills a large place that look'd nobly and stood very high like a large town; they told me it was called either Stowle [Southwold] or Nole I cannot tell which.

I rode in sight of St. Georges Channell in the way from Colchester and Ipswitch and so to Norwich, sometimes it was in view and then lost againe; to Beckle [Beccles] is 8 mile more which in all was 36 miles from Ipswitch – but exceeding long miles – they do own they are 41 measured miles; this is a little market town but its third biggest town in the County of Suffolke, Ipswitch, Berry [Bury St. Edmunds] and this;

Christopher Morris, (ed), The Journeys of Celia Fiennes, 1698, (1949), pp. 144-145.

A Bad Turnpike Road : 1769

The Turnpike between Sudbury and Bury was established in 1762, with a toll house at Sicklesmere. Perhaps there were insufficient funds by 1769 to have improved most of the road.

Much more to be condemned, is the execrable muddy road from Bury to Sudbury in Suffolk; in which I was forced to move as slow as in any unmended land in Wales: for ponds of liquid dirt, and a scattering of loose flints, just sufficient to lame every horse that moves near them, with the addition of cutting vile grips across the road, under pretence of letting water off, but without the effect, all together render, at least, 12 out of these 16 miles, as infamous a turnpike as ever was travelled. Arthur Young, Six Weeks Tour Through The Southern Counties, *(1769), pp. 306-307.*

The Road from Sudbury to Bury St. Edmunds

Dickens describes the same road nearly 70 years later. But he concentrates on the view of the countryside from the coach, rather than the road surface. However, it must have improved, as Mr. Pickwick arrived safely at The Angel.

As the coach rolls swiftly past the fields and orchards which skirt the road, groups of women and children, piling the fruit in sieves, or gathering the scattered ears of corn, pause for an instant from their labour, and shading the sun-burnt face with a still browner hand, gaze upon the passengers with curious eyes, while some stout urchin, too small for work, but too mischievous to be left at home, scrambles over the side of the basket in which he has been deposited for security, and kicks and screams with delight. The reaper stops in his work, and stands with folded arms, looking at the vehicle as it whirls past; and the rough cart-horses bestow a sleepy glance upon the smart coach team, which says, plainly as a horse's glance can, 'It's all very fine to look at, but slow going, over a heavy field, is better than warm work like that, upon a dusty road, after all.' You cast a look behind you as you turn a corner of the road. The women and children have resumed their labour: the reaper once more stoops to his work: the cart-horses have moved on: and all are again in motion.

The influence of a scene like this, was not lost upon the well-regulated mind of Mr. Pickwick...

'Delightful prospect, Sam,' said Mr. Pickwick...

'Beg your pardon, sir, said Sam, suddenly breaking off his loquacious discourse. 'Is this Bury St. Edmunds?'

'It is', replied Mr. Pickwick.

The coach rattled through the well-paved streets of a handsome little town, of thriving and cleanly appearance, and stopped before a large inn situated in a wide open street, nearly facing the old abbey.

'And this,' said Mr. Pickwick, looking up, 'is the Angel! We alight here, Sam.'

Charles Dickens, The Posthumous Papers of the Pickwick Club, *(1837)*.

Needham Market Carrier : 1743

WILLIAM WELLUM: of Needham Market, Carrier. Sets out every Monday Morning at Eight O'clock from the sign of the GUN in Ipswich, for Needham, Stow, Finningham, and Stoke White Horse, and from thence proceed to Norwich, to be there every Wednesday, at the sign of the Pope's Head in the Market Place; and sets out again from the said Place on the Thursday, and comes back the same way, and returns to the Gun at Ipswich on the Friday; by whom all Persons may have any Parcels very safely carried, and at a reasonable Rate.
Ipswich Journal, *15 October 1743.*

Coaching Accident at Beccles : 1788

A most dreadful accident happened on Saturday last at Beccles. As the London coach (by way of Ipswich) was going to Yarmouth, very much loaded with passengers, inside and out, it was overset in passing through that town, by which accident a young woman was killed on the spot, being thrown with such violence against a house, as to break her neck: another woman was so much bruised, that her life is despaired of: a child also had its teeth knocked out, and was otherwise much cut and bruised; the rest of the passengers providentially received little or no injury. What adds to the melancholy fate of the unfortunate young woman is, she was shortly to have been married to a sailor who was then on the roof of the coach, and consequently spectator of the melancholy catastrophe which suddenly thus befell the unhappy object of his expected union.

Surely the above shocking accident, in addition to may others of the like kind, that happen thro' the over-loading stage coaches with outside passengers (for there was no less than 17 in the whole) ought to operate most effectually with the legislature, and induce them unanimously to support Mr. Gamen's Bill brought into the House on Thursday last, for limiting the number of outside passengers on stage coaches.

Bury and Norwich Post, *21 May 1788*.

The Winter of 1836

The snow commenced falling two days before Christmas, and continued for nearly a week, putting a stop to all business in the country, and in some cases there was no communication between towns in Suffolk for five or six days. There was a strong N.E. wind, which laid the high land bare, and gorged the narrow roads and valleys with snow. Between Yoxford and Halesworth, the drifts were in some places from 15 to 20 feet high. Christmas fell on a Sunday, and on the following Tuesday the 'Shannon' coach tried to make the journey from Ipswich to Yarmouth. The roads were bad enough anywhere, but beyond Saxmundham the coach met with extraordinary obstructions. Nine horses were attached to it, but its progress was slow, and in Brake's Lane, near Yoxford, it became so deeply embedded in the snow that it had to be abandoned. Two days afterwards it was dug out, arriving at Halesworth on the Friday. Gangs of 20 or 30 men were employed to clear the roads. There was no communication from Bury to Ipswich from Sunday, the 25th, to Thursday, the 29th, when a man on a horse brought the mail bags, and on the next day, Friday, the time occupied in travelling the distance by coach was eight hours. Except where the wind had cleared the road, there was no passage for vehicles, and a way had to be cut through the snow for traffic. On the Thursday a van drawn by four horses was seven hours on the journey from Needham to Ipswich, a distance of eight miles.

Of course the mails were entirely disorganised. Taking Woodbridge as an example, on Sunday and Monday there were no letters from Norwich, Yarmouth, Cambridge, or Bury St. Edmunds. From Ipswich the letters were conveyed by a man on horseback. The Guard of the Yarmouth Mail had a perilous journey when he did start. Finding it impossible to proceed with the coach, he exchanged it as soon as he could for a post-chaise. In some places the snow was too much even for this, and the bags had alternately to be conveyed by men and horses. In this way they were enabled to leave the main roads and cross fields to avoid the drifts. He arrived at Woodbridge 16 hours behind time, much fatigued and bruised by repeated tumbles.

John Glyde, The Autobiography of a Suffolk Farm Labourer, Suffolk Mercury, *1894–95.*

Ipswich Wants a Railway

Ipswich was thwarted in its desire for a railway in 1843, as the Eastern Counties line from London only reached Colchester. A committee of mainly Suffolk men led by John Cobbold, founded the Eastern Union Railway, to link Ipswich with Colchester, then Bury and Norwich. This rousing verse must be recited loudly and with vigour.

'Rouse ye, rouse ye, men of Ipswich
Up and stirring be the cry
Trade declining, commerce failing,
Seems a threatened danger nigh.

When the spacious dock was forming
What was speculation's view?
Foresight saw the wealth accruing
From a railway passing through

But the line must be diverted
Cries an opposition now;
To the plan by us submitted
Ipswich must submissive bow.

Shall we then, in listless quiet
Let opposing views prevail
See the town and borough dwindle
Down into the lowest scale?

Railways are a stream of traffic
Flowing on with ceaseless tide
Causing riches and extending
Wealthy stores on every side.

Men of Ipswich, as you value
Worth of mercantile renown
Be by bond of union acting
Claim a railway through your town'.

Ipswich Journal, *16 June 1843.*

Opening of the Railway from Ipswich to Colchester : 1846

The last paragraph of this newspaper account with its boom, haugh, haugh and wiz, wiz, could almost have been the inspiration for Thomas The Tank Engine.

The morning of Thursday dawned cheerily, and presaged a delightful trip. Up went the Royal colours at St, Mary-le-Tower Church, at the Custom-house, and at various other points; not forgetting the Wet Dock, where the craft of every degree exhibited their ensigns to the passing breeze, presenting altogether a very gay and animated appearance. The ears of the holiday people were soon afterwards greeted by peals from St. Mary-le-Tower bells, and their festive melodies were borne far and wide. Preparations for giving due éclat to the great event, were soon proceeding on every hand – the programme of the day's sports, consisting of balloon ascent, regatta, cricket, aquatic excursions, cum multis aliis. Indeed the spirit of the Eastern Union Company pervaded all the classes, rich and poor, gentle and simple, old and young.

And a more splendid and imposing 'opening' was never before made by any Railway Company in the kingdom. Neither pains nor expense were spared, whether as it regarded artificial skill, or the liberality with which the Company made every provision to impart to the ceremony due éclat. The Station and other buildings, whether completed or in progress of erection, were gaily decorated with national Standards, Union Jacks, and festoons of laurels and flowers also met the eye in every direction. At the point of junction with the Bury St. Edmunds line, a noble triumph arch was erected, and opposite this spot, a gallery capable of affording accommodation to 600 of the fairer portion of creation, was provided. Both were also decked with a profusion of laurels and flowers, and were surmounted with numerous silken streamers. The whole had a very pretty effect. Towards ten o'clock great crowds of people began to assemble and every available spot for obtaining a glimpse of the train was occupied. Their curiosity was soon gratified. Two of the Company's noble engines, with 13 carriages, including seven of the first class, were drawn out upon the line. The whole were decorated with laurels, flowers, and Union Jacks, and red and white streamers, which unfolded themselves to the breeze in gay and glittering confusion. In an open truck a fine brass band was stationed . . .

The first indications of the start, were screams from the whistles of the engines, and then a pause, and the whole train was then just perceived to be gently and smoothly in motion. At this moment, the clouds dispersed and the sun shone out brilliantly, and the whole scene became one of almost surpassing interest. The band struck up the national Anthem – boom! went the cannon stationed on the western side of the line – loud were the hurras from the crowds in front of the station, answered by the hurras of the crowds at other points – bland were the smiles of the tier upon tier of elegantly dressed and beautiful women who occupied the gallery, as they waved their snowy 'kerchiefs – boom! went the cannon stationed on the dock – enthusiastic were the shouts which again rose from the vast multitude – haugh! haugh! Went the locomotives – whiz! whiz! went the steam, and the whole gained the requisite momentum, when at 10.25 by Ipswich time, the first train that ever left Ipswich speeded majestically on its road to Colchester.

Ipswich Journal, 20 June 1846.

The Last Haverhill Coach

On Saturday last, the 15th January, the Haverhill coach closed its career, after having with its predecessors occupied the road for sixty years; so long has Haverhill boasted a coach – it can do so no longer. For sixty years has the old coach served the inhabitants of this little town in her journeys to London, all weathers. ' December's snows and July' pride' have seen her, through bad roads and good, wending her way to and from 'that spot of glory and that world of woe.' She was not a fast coach, the only complaint ever made of her was that she was slow, but if slow she was sure, and always, except in pace, maintained her position in society. That her career had been a profitable one, until the power of steam was invoked against her, the success of her proprietor (the late Mr. Tredgett) could testify; the careful management and good equipment always observed, made the Haverhill coach a pleasurable means of conveyance, except to those whose pace it did not content. Well, Haverhill, you and your coach are separated, 'the last links are broken.' No more shall her expectant passengers view her moving towards their doors, her well-washed panels and brightened harness glittering in the morning sun; no more shall anxious friends, and ostlers (less concerned, but always glad to see her) listen at night for the sound of her wheels, and of the clattering hoofs that merrily draw her along; no more shall thy youngsters, while gazing on, see around her the parting of relations, who, trying to restrain the public expression of thir feelings, succeed but poorly, nor shall they there see the warm welcome given to the friend, and the still warmer given to the long absent child. No, dear old coach, thou wilt no more gladden us with thy welcome form, thy nags will no longer be the subject of loungers' discussion, admiring gazers will not again see John do that turn into the Bell gateway. No, 'tis all past, the old coach has yielded to the power of steam.

Bury and Norwich Post, 26 January 1848.

The Southwold Light Railway

The Southwold Light Railway opened in 1879 and served the seaside town for 50 years. Its erratic timetable and relaxed nature gave rise to a series of humorous stories and postcards – including one with the train halted to enable passengers to pick flowers from the embankment.

Nobody takes the Southwold Railway seriously, except perhaps its own officials; but as the entire personnel of the railway can be counted on the fingers of two hands, the'officials' are in a minority. The entire distance between Halesworth and Southwold is a little over nine miles, but there are three intermediate stations: Walberswick, Blythburgh and Wenhaston. Although there is only one train, which goes backwards and forwards, the company issues an official time-table, but, luckily, on its outside page, they 'do not guarantee that the trains will keep to the time of starting or arriving as mentioned'. At Southwold the one porter generally rings a bell when the train is going to start, and then the loiterers seat themselves; but, if you happen to get left behind it is quite possible to run after the train and catch it up at Walberswick. This has actually been done, but, of course, in very hot weather it is more comfortable to have a seat in one of the tramcar-like carriages.

If the distance covered by this line is but a short one, the scenery is charming. At first, after leaving Halesworth, you pass through a richly cultivated agricultural district, where the golden corn gives promise of an ample harvest. After leaving Blythburgh, however, the surroundings change, and the line traverses a wild bit of moorland, where the heather and heath are purple in the sun, and the scent of the pine trees is wafted in through the open carriage doors. At Walberswick you come in sight of the sea, and, crossing the Blyth, you pass the Southwold golf-links and enter Southwold station.

T. West Carnie, In Quaint East Anglia, (1899), pp. 49–51.

Wickham Market to Saxmundham : 1889

The notion that the A12 was a lonely place in 1889 is almost beyond comprehension.

A short distance from Wickham Market we noticed a five-fingered sign-post. We had never before met one with such an abundant supply of arms, and, strange to say, all the arms were in excellent condition, the inscriptions on each being perfectly legible; would that all sign-posts were as serviceable to the traveller as this! But then in these railway days who ever dreams of going any distance by road...?

As we proceeded along we presently came to the Lion Inn, evidently a decayed coaching house, and looking now sadly desolate in its fallen estate, doing duty as a roadside public. We were on the main high road from London to Yarmouth, erst busy with much traffic and musical with the sound of the frequent coach-horn. Now we had the way all to ourselves; since we left Woodbridge we had met no vehicle of any kind, and the one or two people we did see appeared to be farm labourers going to or from their work. Sadly deserted are the old high roads, amongst the most lonely places in the land.

Then on through shady woods our way led us to a very pretty little hamlet, the name of which was not given on our map; the village school here [Benhall] with its yellow thatched roof and quaint bell turret tempted us to pull up and make a sketch...

We made our midday halt at Saxmundham, a quiet little market-town, pleasantly situated in the midst of a well-wooded country, one of those picturesque old-fashioned places that in a commercial age are so charmingly uncommercially unprogressive, and unspoilt by growing suburbs; looking now, doubtless, much as it did a century ago, and as in all probability it will look a century hence. A slumberous town that wakes up into some semblance of activity one day in seven, when the market is held there, and farmers and their wives jog in from the country round to do a little business and a good deal of gossip. An uneventful existence these Saxmundhams appear to lead, but a comfortable and contented one withal, untroubled by the keen competitive spirit of the age.

James Hissey, A Tour in a Phaeton, *(1889), pp. 144–46.*

Reader
Pause at this Humble Stone
it Records
The fall of unguarded youth
By the allurements of vice
and the treacherous snares
of Seduction
SARAH LLOYD.
On the 23 of April 1800 in the 22 year of her Age
Suffer'd a just but ignominious
Death,
for admitting her abandoned Seducer
into the dwelling House of
her Mistress
In the night of 3 Oct. 1799.
and becoming the instrument in his hands
of the Crimes of Robbery and House burning
These wretches last Words
May my example be A WARNING
To Thousands.

14 · EPITAPHS

These epitaphs cover the period 1534 – 1884, and record 'all sorts and conditions of men and women.' Here are devoted husbands, virtuous wives, bereft parents; humour based on the deceased's names; the pride of reaching old age; the tradesmen's verses; the details of family history: the plea that the grave may not be disturbed and the warning to be prepared for sudden death.

Four of these stand out for me – Edward Lamb (1647) and the example of his life; the obviously then unusual double grave of Ann and Thomas Hudson (1673); the amazing life and death of Bridgett Applewhaite (1737) and the religious testimony of John Last (1843) which sounds like a personal statement of faith prior to adult baptism in a Nonconformist chapel.

Contynuall prayse these lynes in brasse
Of Allaine Dister here
A clothier virtuous while he was
In Lavenham many a yeare.
For as in lyefe he loved best
The pore to clothe and feede,
So with the riche and all the rest
He neighbourlie agreed;

And did appoynte before he dyed,
A speciall yearly rent,
Which shoulde be every Whitsontide,
Among the poorest spent.
He died 1534.

Lavenham

Here lyeth John and Alice Greene the children of
Robert Greene gent. who died in July 1629—Alice
on the 22 and John on the last daye,
his age was three, hirs twoe yeres old.
Two infant saynts this marble shrine doth keep,
By gentle death in cradle rockt a sleep.
Blest souls no sooner hatchd but lapwinge wyse,
Leaving their earthly neast they mount the skyse.
A hundredth yeres some sunn in vayne, not soe
These clymee to heaven ere they can scarcely goe
The way she leads he kindly hasts as one
To helpe the babe who cold not go alone.

Rishangles

Edward	Edward Lambe	Lambe
Ever	second sonne of	Lived
Envied,	Thomas Lambe,	Laudably
Evill	of Trimley	Lord
Endured	Esquire	Lett
Extremities	All his days	Like
Even	he lived a Batchelor	Life
Earnestly	well learned in devyne	Learne
Expecting	and Common Laws	Lewd
Eternal	with his councell he	Livers
Ease.	helped many, yet took	Lament.
	fees scarce of any.	
	He dyed the 19 November, 1647.	

East Bergholt

Tho Hudson dyed Septr. 5, 1677.
Ann Hudson dyed Octob. 5, 1673
The bodyes of two lovers lyeth here,
Who when alive loved each other dear;
That although death a Separation made,
Yet in one grave together they were laid;
For the first dying, he loving her so
Caused ye Clerke to dig ye grave so low
That above her he might take rest,
And be inclosed in one earthern chest;
And so now resteth here the Twain
Until that God shall raise them up Again.

Woolpit

To free me from domestic strife
Death call'd at my house, but he spake with my wife.
Susan wife of David Patison lies here
       October 19, 1706.
Stop, reader, and if not in a hurry drop a tear.

Hadleigh

      Elizabeth, the wife of
      Thomas Brinkley, died
      24th Feb., 1730, aged 30.
The dame that takes her rest within this tomb,
Had Rachel's face, and Leah's fruitful womb;
Abigail's wisdom, Lydia's faithful heart,
Martha's just care, and Mary's better part.

Woodbridge

John Scarlett. Decoyman. Aged 72.
Died Dec. 31, 1791.
      Contentment is wealth.

Iken

Here lieth Lettice Manning,
Who died 11th of July 1737, aged 49 years.
Oh! Cruel death to please thy Palate
Cut down Lettice to make a Sallet.
Also of Margaret Lot, who died
12th of September, 1748, aged 48 years.
Farewell vain world, I've seen enough of ye,
And now am Careless what thou say of me.
Thy smiles I court not, nor thy frown I fear,
My life is past, my head lie quiet here.

Moulton

To the memory of Peter Gedge
Printer, who first established the
Newspaper published in this Town
He died January 7, 1818, aged 56 years.
Like a worn-out type
He is returned to the founder,
In hopes of being recast
In a better and more perfect mould.

St Marys, Bury

Eliza Gathercole, died 14th Jan., 1848, aged 64.
Our life hangs by a single thread,
Which soon is cut, and we are dead;
Then boast not, reader, of thy might:
Alive at noon and dead at night.

Bury St. Edmunds

William Charles, eldest son of Charles & Emily Denny,
Died at Parham, 9 Aug., 1884, aged 26.
I left my home in perfect health
And little thought that I,
Should from a heavy fall!
So shortly have to die.

Battisford

Between the remains of her brother EDWARD
And of her husband ARTHUR,
Here lies the body of BRIDGETT APPLEWHAITE,
Once BRIDGETT NELSON;
After the fatigues of a married life,
Borne by her with incredible patience
For four years and three-quarters, bating three weeks,
And after the enjoyment of the glorious freedom
Of an easy and unblemisht widowhood
For four years and upwards.
She resolved to run the risk of a second marriage bed,
But DEATH forbad the banns;
And having with an apoplectick dart,
(The same instrument with which he had formerly
Despatched her mother),
Touched the most vital part of her brain.
She must have fallen directly to the ground,
(As one thunder strook),
If she had not been catch't and supported
By her intended husband;
Of which invisible bruise,
After a struggle for above sixty hours
With that grand enemy to life,
(But the certain and merciless friend to helpless old age),
In terrible convulsions, plaintive groans, or stupefying sleep,
Without recovery of her speech or senses,
She died, on the 12th day of Sept., in the year of our Lord,
1737
And of her own age 44.
Behold! I come as a Thief: Rev: 16th Ch: 15th v.
But Oh! Thou source of pious cares
Strict judge without regard
Grant, tho' we go hence unawares,
We go not unprepared.

Bramfield

Phillip Pilbrow, died 18 June, 1750, aged 101.
There are few that do my years exceed,
I to the last, the smallest print could read;
I ne'er was Blooded, nor did Physic try,
God gave me health to live, to him I die.

Ixworth

In memory of John Catchpole,
Who died the 16th of June 1787, aged 75 years.
My horses have done Running,
My wagon is decay'd,
And now in the Dust my body is lay'd.
My whip is worn out, and my work it is done,
And now I'm bought here to my last home.

Palgrave

In a Vault beneath
Are deposited the Remains
Of ANN, the beloved wife
Of JOHN CARTER, of Ipswich, Gent:
And Daughter of the Revd. Denny Cole,
Of this Parish
Who died in Childbed, March 16th, 1790,
Aged 30 years.
How dear the Purchase! How severe the Cost!
The Fruit was sav'd, the parent Tree was lo
This Monumental Shrine, these plaintive Lays,
This sad last Gift a weeping husband pays:
Not that thy Praises, virtuous Fair, require
The breathing Marble or the vocal Lyre,
But as a small, a just return for Love
Tender, unfeign'd and ratify'd above.

Pettistree

Reader
Pause at this Humble Stone
It recalls the fall of unguarded youth
By the allurements of Vice
and the treacherous snares
of Seduction.
SARAH LLOYD
On the 23 of April 1800 in the 22 year
of her age, suffered a just but
ignominious Death
For admitting her abandoned Seducer
into the dwelling house of her Mistress
in the night of 3 October 1799
And becoming the instrument in his hands
of the Crimes of Robbery and House-burning
These were her last Words
May my example be A WARNING
To Thousands.
Bury St. Edmunds

In memory of Dan Calver, who died June 13, 1809,
aged 77 years.
My Sledge and Hammer has reclined,
My Bellows, too, have lost their wind,
My Fires extinct, my Forge decayed,
and in the Dust my Vice is laid.   .
My Coals are spent, my Irons are gone,
My Nails are drove, my Work is done.
A similar epitaph at Hadleigh adds:
My fire-dried corpse lies here at rest
My soul, smoke-like, is soaring to be blest]
Flixton

SACRED

To the memory of JOHN LAST, Farmer of this parish
Who once afar off, was made nigh by the blood of Christ,
And found pardon, peace, and victory over sin,
BY LOOKING UNTO JESUS.
The grace of our lord
Was exceeding abundant towards him.
A father to the poor, lowly in his own eyes,
And making much of them that fear the Lord.
His conversation was in Heaven,
Whither he departed to be with Christ,
Novmber 27th, 1843, aged 64.

Otley.

Short Lived Tenure in St. Clement's Churchyard : 1831

Sat. July 23 1831. The churchyard is kept in a very bad state; numerous footpaths cross it, boys are constantly playing, & it is made the drying ground for all the neighbouring inhabitants; the consequence is that the tombs are broken down, the inscriptions defaced, & in a very few years many of them must become illegible, & many entirely removed. Many of the stones formerly covering table Monuments, are now laid on the ground; and the ch. Yard is so inadequate to the number of Inhabitants, that the Clerk assured me that few bodies remained in the ground more than 7 or 8 years, before they were disturbed to make room for others; fortunately the soil is such that, decomposition is very quick; an instance I saw myself, while I was in the churchyard; the Clerk was digging a grave, from which he turned up a body, certainly far advanced towards dust again, but still in such a state, as to render the disturbing of it, in my eyes, a matter of great indecency: & the mode in which the gravedigger foisted the bones, & the indifference with which he seemed to throw them out, with parts of the coffin not entirely consumed, added no little to my sense of indelicacy of the act.

John Blatchly (ed), A Journal of Excursions Through the County of Suffolk, 1823–25, Suffolk Record Society, vol. xxiv, (1982), p. 172.

ACKNOWLEDGEMENTS

I am grateful to the following for allowing the inclusion of both prose and poetry which remains in copyright: Longman, Green & Co for an extract from *Here we are together* by Robert Arbib; Faber and Faber and Martin Bell for pieces used from *A Street in Suffolk* by Adrian Bell : *Suffolk Prospect* by Justine and Edith Brooke (for which thanks are also due to Edith Brooke's grandson, Chris Hollingsworth, and *Ask the Fellows who cut the hay* and *The Horse in the Furrow* by George Ewart Evans; Boydell and Brewer and the Suffolk Record Society for the *Journal of Excursions of David Davy*; Bowdell and Brewer for an extract from *Suffolk in the Middle Ages* by Norman Scarfe; Hodder and Stoughton Ltd and Norman Scarfe for a piece from Norman Scarfe's *The Suffolk Landscape*; Penguin Books and David Higham Associates for an extract from *Akenfield* by Ronald Blyth; David Desmond and Suffolk Preservation Society for 'The Landscape' in *Suffolk for Ever*, edited by Celia Jennings; Roy Tricker for an excerpt from *Anglicans on High*; Barbara Hopkinson Books for two extracts from *Suffolk Tales* by H.M. West; Professor Francois Lafitte for the Havelock Ellis's *My Life* extract; G.J. Jobson for extracts from Allan Jobson's *Suffolk Yesterday* (Heath Cranton), *North East Suffolk* (Coldharbour) and *This Suffolk* (Heath Cranton); and Neville Turner of Elveden for T.W. Turner's *Memoirs of a gamekeeper*.

I am also grateful to Suffolk Record Office for extracts from documents in their custody.

The publishers have endeavoured to correct all holders of copyright, but will be pleased to add any omissions or correct any errors in future editions.

The front cover shows a detail from *Golding Constable's Flower Garden*, 1815, by John Constable (1776-1837), courtesy of Ipswich Borough Council Museums and Galleries, and for which thanks are due to Sally Dummer, the Registrar and Collections Manager.